AWESOME
ICE POPS

AWESOME
ICE POPS

ANDREW CHASE

Robert
ROSE

For complete cataloguing information, see page 176.

Disclaimer
The recipes in this book have been carefully tested by our kitchen and our tasters. To the best of our knowledge, they are safe and nutritious for ordinary use and users. For those people with food or other allergies, or who have special food requirements or health issues, please read the suggested contents of each recipe carefully and determine whether or not they may create a problem for you. All recipes are used at the risk of the consumer.

We cannot be responsible for any hazards, loss or damage that may occur as a result of any recipe use.

For those with special needs, allergies, requirements or health problems, in the event of any doubt, please contact your medical adviser prior to the use of any recipe.

Editor: Judith Finlayson & Meredith Dees
Proofreader: Gillian Watts
Indexer: Gillian Watts
Recipe tester: Audrey King-Wilson
Design and production: PageWave Graphics Inc.

We acknowledge the support of the Government of Canada.

Canada

Published by Robert Rose Inc.
120 Eglinton Avenue East, Suite 800, Toronto, Ontario, Canada M4P 1E2
Tel: (416) 322-6552 Fax: (416) 322-6936
www.robertrose.ca

Printed and bound in China

1 2 3 4 5 6 7 8 9 ESP 32 31 30 29 28 27 26 25 24

Contents

Introduction

What joy, what freedom, what fun and adventure! During my first school summer break, between kindergarten and first grade, my two sisters and I (ages six and a half, four and five and a half, respectively) were finally allowed to cross busy streets together without the supervision of adults. If we had behaved well enough — that meant essentially that we didn't fight too much for an entire day — we were sometimes rewarded with a quarter, in which case we would set off to the nearest corner store to buy Popsicles. In those days our favorite treat cost seven cents apiece (we used the change to buy penny candies). It was always orange or cherry for me, but I recall that my older sister sometimes had the yellow banana-flavored one or the root beer version, which seemed strange to me; I always felt she was wasting the opportunity to enjoy something better. On rare occasions we split the double Popsicles and shared different flavors while we walked up the hill to our home.

My memories of those childhood excursions are vivid. I can still feel the rush of independence and the indulgence that Popsicles represented to three rather mischievous kids. Those moments are frozen in time (forgive the pun) and often recalled some fifty years later. However, while I know that the first taste of a commercial ice pop might transport my soul to those carefree days, the second lick definitely brings me back to reality: my all-too-adult and more discriminating present. Nowadays I want to make better, tastier, more natural ice pops myself.

Fortunately, it's not hard to make your own ice pops. It's one of the quickest and easiest ways to satisfy your family and friends with real homemade treats. Years after our childhood trips to the corner store, our mother bought some simple ice pop molds and just froze orange juice on sticks. In those days it didn't occur to any of us to do more to brighten up the flavor — ice cold and fruity was enough to beat the summer heat. But now we tend to enjoy frozen treats year-round, and we are more demanding about everything we eat, especially things that fall into the category of indulgence. It's precisely because ice pops aren't essential that they should be fun and exciting, extremely flavorful and available in as many varieties as possible. From simple and straightforward to rich and luxurious, the one thing they should have in common is delicious, extravagant flavor.

In putting together this collection of recipes, I have strived to cover all the bases. I pursued delicious presentations of as many different kinds of fruit as was practically possible. I aspired to fully satisfy chocolate lovers and caramel fanatics, to give pleasure to those who love spices and to appease those whose main culinary concern is healthy eating. North American, East Asian, Southeast Asian, Latin American, Mediterranean and Indian flavors, among others, are explored. If you are feeding toddlers and small children, you can offer them healthy ice pops, while their relaxed parents can enjoy adult versions flavored like cocktails.

I am confident that everyone will find some favorite familiar flavors to enjoy. At the same time, I hope you will be enticed to try some of the more exotic offerings. That's the fun of food in our times: discovering new and exciting flavors from around the world while embracing our beloved local and seasonal foods.

In this book, including variations, I've created more than 75 recipes for ice pops — surely enough variety for everyone. In my opinion, each one is as tasty and fun as the next. So, relive your youth! Indulge yourself, your children, your friends and your family! In other words, enjoy making, serving and eating these ice pops.

_ Andrew Chase

Ice pops can be
icy and light or
rich and smooth.

All About Ice Pops

Ice pops are frozen treats on a stick. This is the definition I have used to mark the boundaries of this book. They are not ice cream or ice cream bars, they are not sorbets or sherbets, and they are not mousses frozen on a stick. Yet this narrow definition allows for a huge variety of delicious frozen treats.

Ice pops can be icy and light or rich and smooth. Some are as sweet as candy, others are mouth-puckeringly tart, and some are even savory. There are many ice pops made from fruit, while others embrace chocolate and cream or nuts and seeds. Some find their inspiration in coffee or tea, others in cocktails or punches. There are even ice pops made from vegetables and legumes.

Ice pops are popular all over the world, anywhere where summers are hot and refrigeration is possible. But no matter what their origin or their ingredients, ice pops are first and foremost treats, and they are all made from liquid mixtures that are frozen solidly onto a stick.

Fruit

If you need one good reason to make ice pops, it's fruit. Using the ripest, freshest fruit, you can craft treats that are a frozen expression of a fruit's essence. Like other frozen fruit preparations or chilled desserts, ice pops can give a boost to the natural flavors of fruits, intensifying them through simple preparation methods and broadening them by adding complementary flavors. To develop a fruit ice pop recipe, I aim to get at the heart of the fruit — to enhance, not alter, its essence. Added sweetness, tartness and seasoning are there to highlight the original flavor.

And what an array of fruit there is! From the chilly fringes of its temperate zones to the hottest jungles of the tropics, the world is awash in fruit. That's good news for me, because I doubt there is a single palatable fruit that cannot be turned into a delicious ice pop.

Freshness and **ripeness** are essential. It is important that you find the best fruit you can to make ice pops. No matter how much you manipulate it, unripe or poor-quality fruit will give a disappointing result. Ice pops are a great way to use ripe fruit at its peak, especially in the summer and autumn months, when we tend to get overwhelmed by the quality and quantity of fruit available. Out of peak season, don't overlook **frozen fruit**, which is usually harvested at the peak of ripeness and then flash-frozen.

Lemons and limes are particularly important for making fruit-based ice pops. Besides being the base fruit for lemon- or lime-flavored ice pops, these fruits are essential flavoring agents in almost all fruit-based ice pops. The zest of both (as well as other citrus fruits) livens up syrups and fruit purées, and their tart juices balance the natural sugars in other fruits. Balancing sweetness in fruit mixtures with some natural acidity is necessary for good, well-rounded flavor. Always use **freshly squeezed** lemon juice or lime juice for your ice pops; bottled juice just doesn't compare. For other citrus juices, such as orange and grapefruit, freshly squeezed is of course the best, but fresh juice from cartons or from concentrate can also be used.

Citrus zest (rind) is used extensively in this cookbook as a flavoring for ice pops of all descriptions. For recipes that include citrus zest, I recommend using organic produce, which should have substantially fewer potentially harmful residues from agricultural sprays. All citrus fruit should be well rinsed and dried before use.

CITRUS ZEST

When a recipe calls for citrus zest, it means the colored part of the rind only. Avoid grating or cutting off any of the bitter white pith directly under the zest.

Dairy and Chocolate

After fruit pops, dairy and chocolate ice pops are the largest category in this book. They range from familiar fudge and orange cream ice pops to traditional Indian kulfi and Korean-style melon cream ice pops. Unlike ice creams, which are churned to achieve a smooth, soft texture, dairy ice pops must freeze solidly on their sticks. The texture is icier, with bigger crystals than ice cream. You can, of course, freeze ice cream on a stick, but that's an ice cream bar, not a proper ice pop. All the dairy ice pops in this book celebrate their "ice pop–ness" with their unique textures and flavors.

Sweeteners

Every ice pop needs a judicious amount of sweetening to be palatable. A great many sweeteners are used in the recipes. Plain white granulated **sugar** is perhaps the most common because it is the most neutral in flavor and often the best sugar for clear syrups. However, I have used many other kinds of sugar to take advantage of the wide range of flavors they offer, from moist, dark demerara to clear, light yellow rock sugar.

Flavoring Ice Pops

Freezing adds its own challenges to flavoring. Although every recipe in this book is well tested, the sweetness, ripeness and flavor levels of your fruit and other ingredients may vary slightly, so I always encourage tasting and adjusting to taste. However, don't judge the flavor of your mixtures while they are still warm. Wait until they reach room temperature or, better still, place them in the refrigerator to cool.

Here are a few guidelines for flavoring ice pops:

- Err on the sweet side. Freezing diminishes the level of sweetness in an ice pop mixture.
- Use a light hand with spices. They mysteriously gain strength after freezing, so take a subtle approach.
- Pique the flavor with a pinch of salt. If your fruit mixture seems a tad bland, try adding just a tiny pinch. The smallest amount is often enough to perfectly enhance the flavor of fruit.

USE THE BEST INGREDIENTS

As with any kind of cooking, your ice pops will only be as good as your ingredients. Try to use the best ingredients you can find: the ripest and tastiest fruit, the finest chocolate, the richest dairy products, the freshest herbs and spices. You will be rewarded with standout ice pops — treats that are certainly worth the effort.

I recommend keeping several different varieties of **honey** in your pantry, because using different honeys is an easy way to vary the flavor of ice pops. Prepared **syrups** such as light agave, brown rice, malt or maple syrup can also make an important contribution; they improve the texture of ice pops, creating a softer and less icy mouth-feel. In addition, many contribute valuable flavors of their own.

Coatings

If you are so inclined, you can coat the outside of your ice pop, in whole or in part, with various toppings. Chopped nuts, flaked or shredded coconut, candy bits, sprinkles, cookie crumbs and sesame and other seeds are all appropriate coatings. Just dip or brush a solidly frozen ice pop with a little syrup, juice, liqueur or spirit to taste and sprinkle on the topping.

TO COAT AN ICE POP IN CHOCOLATE, you must ensure that your ice pop is fully frozen, so let it freeze overnight. You will need about $1^1/_2$ ounces (45 g) chocolate per $^1/_4$ to $^1/_3$ cup (60 to 75 mL) ice pop mixture. Melt the chocolate in a heatproof bowl over barely simmering water. For a shinier coating that's just a touch softer, stir in $^1/_2$ tsp (2 mL) corn or agave syrup. After melting, remove the chocolate from the water bath and set aside to cool to room temperature. When the chocolate has cooled, dip in your frozen ice pop to coat. To set the chocolate, insert the ice pop stick in a Styrofoam block or flower-arranging foam and freeze upright until it is firm.

Alcohol and Ice Pops

Alcoholic beverages such as rum and brandy are used as flavoring in the occasional ice pop recipe. Because alcohol has a low freezing temperature, when it is used in an ice pop recipe, the texture is affected. I've added a small shot of neutral vodka to a few recipes to keep the ice pops from freezing too hard; if you wish, the alcohol can be left out. Rum extract can replace the flavor of real rum in some cases, as noted in the recipes.

COCKTAIL ICE POPS: Where alcohol is an integral component of an ice pop, it's important to keep the ratio down. Alcohol (40 percent/80 proof) should not comprise more than one part in five, or 20 percent of the volume. Otherwise the mixture will not freeze solidly. When making cocktail ice pops, it is best to let them freeze overnight to ensure that they set properly. All the cocktail ice pops will have a softer and smoother texture than those that don't contain alcohol, and you must take some care when unmolding them — the sticks are more likely to twist out and the ice pop will be more inclined to break in the mold.

Using the ripest, freshest fruit, you can craft treats that are a frozen expression of a fruit's essence.

Embellishing Ice Pops

Given all the recipes in this book, you might be wondering what else you could do with ice pops, but there is always room to gild the lily, so to speak. There are numerous ways of embellishing your ice pops for original presentation, for parties or just for fun.

LAYERED ICE POPS: Try to make layered ice pops of your own invention. Almost all the fruit mixtures would taste good layered with other flavors, and many of the dairy and chocolate recipes could also be layered successfully. Just pick two or three compatible recipes and halve or reduce the amounts proportionally, or plan on making a double (or triple) batch of pops. To layer ice pops, you don't need any special equipment or even any special skill. All you need is patience: each layer must be well frozen before another layer is added, and it will take at least 30 to 60 minutes to freeze hard enough. So make sure you have the time, and don't forget to add the stick after the first layer.

ADDED AND SUSPENDED INGREDIENTS: Some people like to add bits of chopped or sliced fruit, whole small berries, candy bits, nuts, seeds and so on to their ice pops. I'm a bit of a purist and not much of a fan of pieces of frozen fruit or seeds in my ice pops, so I have largely avoided these add-ins. However, ingredients suspended in ice are very attractive visually, so if you are looking for a wow factor in your ice pops, you may want to consider this option.

In general terms, when adding ingredients, stick to add-ins that are directly related to the ingredients in the recipe. For instance, a couple of slices of strawberry suspended in a strawberry ice pop makes sense and looks pretty, as does a slice or two of banana or pineapple in a tropical fruit punch ice pop.

Add-ins can be mixed directly into thicker ice pop mixtures. To suspend them properly in thin mixtures, you must first freeze a layer and then freeze the add-in ingredient(s) in subsequent layers.

Edible flowers and herbs are often added in styled photographs of ice pops, and they look very attractive when frozen. However, flowers may have a wilted mouth-feel when you eat the ice pop, so choose carefully.

Ice Pop Molds

Ice pop making is remarkably simple and straightforward. There are no "trade secrets" when it comes to making these treats.

There are many types of **ice pop molds** on the market. In most things I prefer the uncomplicated and traditional — in this case, nostalgic and familiar round-ended flat ice pop molds. The best are made of durable plastic set in a metal holder, with a metal cover that holds the sticks. Very inexpensive cone- and tube-shaped molds are available in cheaper, less durable plastic and are easy to use too.

Cooking supply shops sell an array of **silicone ice pop molds**. These are extremely easy to unmold but are usually sold in fairly expensive sets that make just a few ice pops each. **Wax-lined paper cups** (often called "bathroom cups") make simple and useful throwaway molds. These are small cups that hold about $1/3$ cup (75 mL), like the kind used in dentist's offices. Make sure they are actually wax-lined or you will have a horrible time unmolding the ice pops. You must ensure that you have a strong, flat base to rest your cups on in the freezer.

Pricey **ice pop makers** that you store in your freezer are also available. The advantage is that they make almost instant ice pops (in less than 10 minutes). However, they can make only a few at a time.

STICKS FOR ICE POPS

I prefer simple, traditional wooden sticks to all others. I like the rounded tips and the way they absorb liquid so that they expand and adhere securely to the frozen filling. They are cheap and plentiful, feel good to hold, are disposable and biodegradable, and don't have to be retrieved and washed (which is especially important for picnics and for ice pops that will be served to children), unlike the special sticks that come with fancier molds.

Filling, Freezing and Unmolding Ice Pops

FILLING THE MOLDS: Don't fill them all the way to the top. Leave a little bit of room — at least $1/4$ inch (0.5 cm) — for expansion from inserting the stick and the natural expansion from freezing.

INSERTING STICKS: The easiest method by far is to leave the molds uncovered and insert the sticks after the mixture has frozen to a slushy consistency (usually after about 90 minutes). Some people soak the sticks in water first to prevent them from floating, but I find that unnecessary, and any extra wet sticks will be susceptible to mold.

If you don't have time to pre-freeze the mixture, you may need a metal lid to hold the sticks securely in the molds, or you can cover the top of your molds with aluminum foil and make slits to hold the sticks in place. Make sure the sticks are straight and stay that way, especially when using a multiple mold with a metal lid; the stiff lid can be very difficult to remove if the sticks are wonky.

FREEZING: Set your freezer thermostat for a cold temperature and make sure you have a clear, flat place to put the molds. Most freezers will take at least four hours to freeze non-alcoholic ice pops, but longer is always better.

UNMOLDING: Quickly run hot water over the outside of the mold and then pull out the ice pops without twisting (which can loosen the sticks).

STORING: Wrap individual ice pops tightly in plastic wrap and store in sealable freezer bags. They keep for several weeks or longer, provided that your freezer maintains a steady cold temperature.

Basic Tools for Making Ice Pops

Large Pyrex measuring cups with spouts are extremely convenient for making ice pops. Not only can you measure your ingredients, if you use a large measuring cup to hold the entire mixture you can quickly calculate exactly how many pops it will make. Also, the pouring spout makes it easy to pour directly into the molds. Most blender containers also have measurement markings and good spouts for pouring, so it isn't necessary to pour the mixture into a measuring cup if it is finished in the blender.

A good, strong **blender** is essential for making some of the recipes. Every brand of blender has a different power capacity, so the speeds vary greatly. Generally, to purée a mixture, start at a slow to medium speed and then move up to medium-high (with a powerful blender) or high speed (with a less powerful model). If the engine is very strong, too much air may be incorporated into a mixture at high speed. For blending mixtures that don't need to be entirely smooth or with small seeds that you don't want to break up, slow to medium speeds (or medium-high on a less powerful blender) are appropriate. Always start blending hot mixtures at the slowest speed and work your way up gradually.

You will also need a strong **fine-mesh sieve** to strain out unwanted solids (seeds, skins, spices and such) as well as to smooth out rougher mixtures. You can use a strong rubber or silicone **spatula**, a **wooden spoon** or a **soup ladle** to push mixtures through a fine sieve.

A good **silicone spatula** is immensely useful, and two are better. I like to use a narrow one for scraping down the blender and a wider one for scraping mixtures through a sieve or getting everything out of mixing bowls and measuring cups. Silicone spatulas are heatproof and nonstick too, so they are good for scraping hot syrup out of a saucepan.

One last bit of advice: **keep a separate cutting board for fruit only**, and rinse it right after use so other flavors will not contaminate your fruit flavors.

A good, strong blender is essential for making some of the recipes.

Fruity

Orangeade
Ice Pops

MAKES ABOUT 2²/₃ CUPS (650 ML) ◆ 8 TO 10 ICE POPS

Orange is the most popular flavor for commercially made ice pops.
The good news is, it's a cinch to make your own all-natural orange ice pops,
which have a more concentrated flavor and much less sugar. Using citrus zest
in the syrup base intensifies the flavor, which is important for frozen treats.

Fine-mesh sieve

1/2 cup (125 mL) granulated sugar

1/2 cup (125 mL) water

Finely grated zest of 2 oranges

2 cups (500 mL) orange juice

1 In a small saucepan, combine sugar, water and orange zest. Bring to a boil, stirring until sugar is dissolved; reduce heat and simmer for 1 minute. Remove from heat and cover; set aside to steep for 5 minutes. Strain through sieve into a large measuring cup. Stir in orange juice.

2 Pour into molds and freeze until slushy, then insert sticks and freeze until solid, for at least 4 hours. If you are using an ice pop kit, follow the manufacturer's instructions.

Tip

Use this recipe to make ice pops from any variety of oranges. Valencia, Hamlin, pineapple or blood (moro), navel or pink-juiced cara cara oranges, as well as mandarin oranges and tangerines. Orange-grapefruit hybrids such as tangelos (Orlando, Minneola or honeybell) also work well.

Orange Cream
Ice Pops

MAKES ABOUT 2¹/₂ CUPS (625 ML) ◆ 7 TO 10 ICE POPS

Intensely orange and creamy at the same time, these are for those who crave the orange-flavored cream pops of their childhood but prefer a more adult flavor.

Finely grated zest of 1 orange

²/₃ cup (150 mL) orange juice

¹/₃ cup + 1 tbsp (90 mL) orange blossom or other light floral honey

¹/₂ cup (125 mL) frozen orange juice concentrate

²/₃ cup (150 mL) heavy or whipping (35%) cream

¹/₃ cup (75 mL) evaporated milk

1 In a small saucepan, combine orange zest and juice and honey. Bring to a boil, reduce heat and simmer for 4 minutes. Remove from heat and set aside to cool slightly. Whisk in concentrate. Pour into a large measuring cup and whisk in cream and milk.

2 Pour into molds and freeze until slushy, then insert sticks and freeze until solid, for at least 4 hours. If you are using an ice pop kit, follow the manufacturer's instructions.

Classic Lemonade
Ice Pops

If you can get your hands on juicy fresh lemons, make lemonade,
of course — or even better, make lemonade ice pops. And if you are
lucky enough to get a bag of Meyer lemons (see Tip, below),
you will end up with the most delicious lemonade ice pops ever!

Fine-mesh sieve

2¹/₂ cups (625 mL) water, divided

²/₃ cup (150 mL) granulated sugar

1 tsp (5 mL) finely grated lemon zest

³/₄ cup (175 mL) freshly squeezed lemon juice

> **VARIATION**
>
> **HONEY LEMONADE ICE POPS:** Reduce sugar to ¹/₄ cup (60 mL). Proceed as above, whisking ¹/₃ cup (75 mL) liquid honey into syrup after straining.

1 In a small saucepan over medium heat, combine ¹/₂ cup (125 mL) water, sugar and lemon zest. Bring to a boil, then reduce heat and simmer for 3 minutes. Set aside to cool. Strain resulting syrup through sieve placed over a large measuring cup, discarding solids. Whisk in lemon juice and remaining 2 cups (500 mL) water.

2 Pour into molds and freeze until slushy, then insert sticks and freeze until solid, for at least 4 hours. If you are using an ice pop kit, follow the manufacturer's instructions.

Tip

Meyer lemons are thin-skinned lemons originally from China. It is thought they were bred from crossing lemons with mandarin or regular oranges. They have a strong floral perfume and slightly sweeter juice than regular lemons. During the winter months they are exported from Florida and California to most North American locations.

Classic Limeade
Ice Pops

MAKES ABOUT 3 CUPS (750 ML) ◆ 9 TO 12 ICE POPS

Use regular large (Persian) limes, Key limes or Mexican limes for this classic.

Fine-mesh sieve

2$\frac{1}{4}$ cups (550 mL) water, divided

$\frac{1}{2}$ cup (125 mL) granulated sugar

$\frac{3}{4}$ tsp (3 mL) finely grated lime zest

$\frac{1}{8}$ tsp (0.5 mL) salt

$\frac{3}{4}$ cup (175 mL) freshly squeezed lime juice

1 In a saucepan over medium heat, combine $\frac{1}{2}$ cup (125 mL) water, sugar, lime zest and salt. Bring to a boil, stirring until sugar dissolves, reduce heat and simmer for 3 minutes. Set aside to cool. Strain syrup through sieve into a large measuring cup. Whisk in lime juice and remaining 1$\frac{3}{4}$ cups (425 mL) water.

2 Pour into molds and freeze until slushy, then insert sticks and freeze until solid, for at least 4 hours. If you are using an ice pop kit, follow the manufacturer's instructions.

Tips

These ice pops are very pale green; intensify the green with a few drops of food coloring, if you have no concerns about potential health issues.

Always use freshly squeezed lemon juice or lime juice in your ice pops; bottled just doesn't compare.

Spicy Lime
Ice Pops

MAKES ABOUT 2 CUPS (500 ML) ◆ 6 TO 8 ICE POPS

These ice pops are an intriguing mix of fruit and spice. Brown rice syrup or agave syrup adds a pleasant undertone of flavor but will slightly darken the mixture, while light corn syrup is clear and virtually tasteless. Choose the one that suits you best.

Fine-mesh sieve

2 tsp (10 mL) finely grated lime zest

2 tbsp (30 mL) granulated sugar

1 1/2 cups (375 mL) cold water

1/2 cup (125 mL) freshly squeezed lime juice

1/3 cup (75 mL) brown rice syrup or 1/4 cup (60 mL) light agave or light corn syrup

1/4 tsp (1 mL) salt

1/4 tsp (1 mL) ground roasted cumin (see Tip, right)

Pinch cayenne pepper

Pinch black pepper

1 In a bowl, mix together lime zest and sugar, pressing down with the back of a spoon to help release the oils in the zest. Stir in water until sugar is dissolved. Let sit for 5 minutes. Strain through sieve placed over a large measuring cup, pressing on solids to extract as much liquid as possible. Discard solids.

2 Stir in lime juice, syrup, salt, cumin, cayenne and black pepper until syrup is thoroughly incorporated.

3 Pour into molds and freeze until slushy, then, with sticks, stir to evenly redistribute spices. Insert sticks and freeze until solid, for at least 4 hours. If you are using an ice pop kit, follow the manufacturer's instructions.

Tip

Ground roasted cumin is a useful ingredient to add to your spice cabinet. It has more flavor than unroasted cumin and it's easy to make: In a dry skillet over medium-low heat, cook cumin seeds until fragrant and lightly toasted, about 2 to 3 minutes. Pound or grind into a powder and store in an airtight container for up to one month.

Peaches and Cream
Ice Pops

MAKES ABOUT 2¹/₂ CUPS (625 ML) ◆ 7 TO 10 ICE POPS

Peaches and cream are a classic combination. Here I've added a few raspberries to pique the flavor and improve the color of the ice pops. Use the freshest and ripest peaches you can find. Out of season, use thawed frozen ripe peaches.

Fine-mesh sieve

Blender, immersion blender or potato masher

2 cups (500 mL) chopped peeled peaches

¹/₃ cup (75 mL) water

¹/₃ cup (75 mL) packed dark brown sugar

¹/₄ cup (60 mL) granulated sugar

3 tbsp (45 mL) fresh or frozen raspberries

²/₃ cup (150 mL) heavy or whipping (35%) cream

¹/₄ tsp (1 mL) vanilla extract

1 In a saucepan, combine peaches, water and brown and granulated sugars. Bring to a boil, stirring until sugar is dissolved. Reduce heat and simmer until peaches are very tender, about 10 minutes. Meanwhile, place raspberries in sieve and immerse in simmering peaches until softened, about 2 minutes. Using a rubber spatula, scrape raspberry pulp and juice through sieve into peach mixture. Discard seeds. Remove from heat and set aside to cool.

2 Once cool, transfer to blender and blend at medium speed until smooth. Add cream and vanilla and pulse to blend.

3 Pour into molds and freeze until slushy, then insert sticks and freeze until solid, for at least 4 hours. If you are using an ice pop kit, follow the manufacturer's instructions.

Tip

Truly ripe peaches should be easy to peel with the side of a sharp knife blade. If, however, the skin is a bit tight, simply plunge the peaches in boiling water for about 10 seconds to loosen the skins.

Lemon Rosemary Pear
Ice Pops

MAKES ABOUT 3 CUPS (750 ML) ◆ 9 TO 12 ICE POPS

The intrinsic pleasure of sweet ripe pears needs merely a boost of acidity and subtle flavoring to transform them into well-balanced and delicious ice pops. In this recipe lemon juice along with a rosemary-scented lemon syrup, does the trick.

Blender

$1^1/_3$ cups (325 mL) water

$^1/_2$ cup (125 mL) granulated sugar

2 strips ($^1/_2$ by 2 inches/1 by 5 cm) lemon zest

$^1/_3$ cup (75 mL) freshly squeezed lemon juice

1 sprig fresh rosemary

$1^1/_2$ lbs (750 g) ripe pears (about 4), peeled, cored and chopped

3 tbsp (45 mL) liquid honey

$^1/_4$ tsp (1 mL) almond extract

1 In a saucepan, combine water, sugar, lemon zest and juice and rosemary. Bring to a boil, stirring until sugar is dissolved; add pears and return to a boil. Reduce heat and simmer until pears are very soft, 10 to 20 minutes, depending on variety and ripeness. Stir in honey and almond extract. Set aside to cool.

2 Discard rosemary sprig and any loose rosemary leaves. Transfer pear mixture to blender and blend at medium-high speed until smooth.

3 Pour into molds and freeze until slushy, then insert sticks and freeze until solid, for at least 4 hours. If you are using an ice pop kit, follow the manufacturer's instructions.

Red Plum
Ice Pops

When cooked in a light syrup, then frozen, red plums have an intense flavor that matches the deep red color of this ice pop.

Fine-mesh sieve

1 lb (500 g) unpeeled red plums (5 large or 8 medium), pitted and chopped

$1/2$ cup (125 mL) water

$1/3$ cup + 1 tbsp granulated sugar

Pinch salt

2 tbsp (30 mL) freshly squeezed lemon juice

1 Place plums in a saucepan with water, sugar and a scant pinch of salt; bring to a boil. Reduce heat and simmer, covered, until fruit is soft, about 10 minutes. Stir in lemon juice.

2 Strain through sieve placed over a large measuring cup, pressing down and scraping solids with a rubber spatula to extract as much pulp and juice as possible. Discard solids. Set aside to cool.

3 Pour into molds and freeze until slushy, then insert sticks and freeze until solid, for at least 4 hours. If you are using an ice pop kit, follow the manufacturer's instructions.

Cherry
Ice Pops

MAKES ABOUT 2¹/₄ CUPS (550 ML) ◆ 6 TO 9 ICE POPS

Unlike artificially flavored commercial ice pops, these ones taste
of real cherries — a beautiful summer treat.

Fine-mesh sieve

3 cups (750 mL) whole sweet cherries
(generous 1 lb/500 g), pitted

1 cup + 2 tbsp (280 mL) water

¹/₂ cup (125 mL) granulated sugar

4 tsp (20 mL) freshly squeezed
lemon juice

1 In a saucepan, combine cherries, water and sugar.
Bring to a boil, stirring until sugar is dissolved, then
reduce heat, cover and simmer until cherries are soft,
about 20 minutes.

2 Strain through sieve placed over a large measuring
cup, pressing down and scraping solids with a rubber
spatula or wooden spoon to extract as much pulp and
juice as possible. Discard skins. Whisk in lemon juice
and set aside to cool.

3 Pour into molds and freeze until slushy, then insert
sticks and freeze until solid, for at least 4 hours. If you
are using an ice pop kit, follow the manufacturer's
instructions.

VARIATIONS

RAINIER CHERRY ICE POPS: Use Rainier cherries
and increase lemon juice to 5
tsp (25 mL). Rainier cherries
are pale yellow, red-splotched
cherries that have a more
delicate flavor and are slightly
sweeter than black cherries.

SOUR CHERRY ICE POPS:
Use pie or sour (tart red)
cherries such as Montmorency
or Morello. Increase sugar to
²/₃ cup (150 mL) for pleasantly
tart ice pops or ³/₄ to 1 cup
(175 to 250 mL), to taste, for
sweet ones.

Kiwi Ginger
Ice Pops

MAKES ABOUT 2¹/₂ CUPS (625 ML) ◆ 7 TO 10 ICE POPS

A ginger syrup highlights the exotic taste of New Zealand's signature fruit.

Blender

Fine-mesh sieve

¹/₂ cup (125 mL) granulated sugar

1¹/₂ tbsp (22 mL) finely grated gingerroot

Pinch salt

³/₄ cup (175 mL) water

5 or 6 kiwifruit

1 In a small saucepan, combine sugar, ginger and a scant pinch of salt. Cook over medium heat until sugar has melted into a completely clear liquid and large bubbles have subsided, 4 to 5 minutes. Stir in water and bring to a boil. Remove from heat and set aside to cool.

2 Peel and halve kiwis lengthwise and cut out any hard cores. Chop enough fruit to make 2 cups (500 mL). Place in blender, then strain ginger syrup through sieve into blender. Discard ginger. Purée mixture at medium-high speed.

3 Pour into molds and freeze until slushy, then insert sticks and freeze until solid, for at least 4 hours. If you are using an ice pop kit, follow the manufacturer's instructions.

Tip

Green kiwifruit give these ice pops a really fabulous look, but for a sweeter and milder taste you can use golden kiwis, which make an attractive yellow ice pop flecked with tiny black seeds.

Watermelon Punch
Ice Pops

MAKES ABOUT 2 CUPS (500 ML) ◆ 6 TO 8 ICE POPS

Incredibly simple to make and very refreshing,
these ice pops score high with both children and adults.

Blender

4 cups (1 L) chopped seedless
(or seeded) watermelon

3 tbsp (45 mL) grenadine syrup
(see Tip, right)

2 tbsp (30 mL) freshly squeezed
lemon juice

1 In blender at medium-high speed, purée watermelon,
grenadine syrup and lemon juice.

2 Pour into molds and freeze until slushy, then insert
sticks and freeze until solid, for at least 4 hours. If you
are using an ice pop kit, follow the manufacturer's
instructions.

Tips

Grenadine syrup is a clear red syrup originally made from
pomegranates (grenades in French) and now often from
a combination of red fruit flavorings. It's what gives this
ice pop its "punch" and its beautiful red color. Look for
it in well-stocked supermarkets or liquor stores.

If your watermelon has soft white immature seeds
embedded in the flesh, then strain mixture through
a fine sieve before pouring into molds.

Minty Honeydew
Ice Pops

MAKES ABOUT 3^1/$_3$ CUPS (825 ML) ◆ 10 TO 13 ICE POPS

Ripe honeydew pairs with fresh mint syrup to make a lovely green, fragrant ice pop. This is a great way to use up abundant mint from your summer garden, just when honeydew melons are also at their best.

Blender

Fine-mesh sieve

^{1}/$_2$ cup (125 mL) rock (yellow crystal) sugar or scant ^{1}/$_2$ cup (125 mL) granulated sugar

^{1}/$_2$ cup (125 mL) water

1 cup (250 mL) lightly packed mint leaves

4 cups (1 L) chopped ripe honeydew melon

2 tbsp (30 mL) freshly squeezed lemon juice

1 In a small saucepan, bring sugar and water to a boil. Reduce heat to medium and simmer, stirring, until sugar is dissolved, about 5 minutes (if using granulated sugar, simmer for 2 minutes). Stir in mint. Cover and set aside to steep for 5 minutes.

2 Transfer to blender and purée at medium-high speed. Strain through sieve without pressing down on solids. Discard solids and set liquid aside.

3 In blender at medium-high speed, purée melon and lemon juice. Strain through sieve placed over a large measuring cup; do not press down on solids, but shake sieve to strain out as much liquid as possible. Discard solids. Whisk reserved mint syrup into melon mixture.

4 Pour into molds and freeze until slushy, then insert sticks and freeze until solid, for at least 4 hours. If you are using an ice pop kit, follow the manufacturer's instructions.

Tip

Rock (yellow crystal) sugar is a clear, light yellow sugar in large crystals used primarily in Chinese cooking. It is slightly less sweet than granulated sugar and makes a clear, shiny syrup. You can purchase it at Asian markets and some large supermarkets. It comes in either large, irregular natural crystals or regular smaller ones, which are obviously easier to measure. If using large crystals, break them up before measuring.

Cantaloupe Fennel
Ice Pops

MAKES ABOUT 2¹/₂ CUPS (625 ML) ◆ 7 TO 10 ICE POPS

These cantaloupe ice pops have a whisper of fennel seed and
a touch of lime — all that's needed if you have a truly ripe melon.

Blender

1 tsp (5 mL) fennel seeds

¹/₂ cup (125 mL) water

¹/₃ cup + 1 tbsp (90 mL) granulated sugar

2 strips (each about ¹/₂ by
1¹/₂ inches/1 by 4 cm) lime zest

3 cups (750 mL) chopped ripe
cantaloupe or musk melon

1¹/₂ tbsp (22 mL) freshly squeezed
lime juice

1 In a small saucepan over medium heat, toast fennel seeds until slightly darkened and fragrant, 2 to 3 minutes. Add water, sugar and lime zest. Bring to a boil, then simmer over medium heat for 3 minutes. Remove from heat and set aside to cool.

2 Strain syrup into blender, discarding seeds and zest. Add melon and purée at medium-high speed.

3 Pour into molds and freeze until slushy, then insert sticks and freeze until solid, for at least 4 hours. If you are using an ice pop kit, follow the manufacturer's instructions.

Tip

A good ripe melon should give slightly to the touch (particularly at the blossom end) and be heavy with juice. If you put your nose close to the blossom end, the melon should smell as sweet as a tropical flower. A melon without a strong fragrance will have little flavor.

Blackberry
Ice Pops

MAKES ABOUT 2¹/₃ CUPS (575 ML) ◆ 7 TO 9 ICE POPS

Blackberries are one of the real pleasures of late summer. Their intensity has always made them popular for sweets, and ice pops are no exception.

Blender

Fine-mesh sieve

1 lb (500 g) blackberries (4 cups/1 L)

1¹/₃ cups (325 mL) unsweetened apple juice

¹/₃ cup (75 mL) granulated sugar

1 tbsp (15 mL) freshly squeezed lemon juice

1 In blender at medium speed, blend blackberries and apple juice until mostly liquid and berries are completely broken up. Scrape into a saucepan and add sugar; stir until dissolved. Bring to a boil and immediately remove from heat. Set aside to cool slightly.

2 Over a large measuring cup, strain blackberry mixture through sieve, pressing down and scraping solids with a rubber spatula to extract as much pulp and juice as possible. Discard seeds. Stir in lemon juice.

3 Pour into molds and freeze until slushy, then insert sticks and freeze until solid, for at least 4 hours. If you are using an ice pop kit, follow the manufacturer's instructions.

Strawberry
Ice Pops

MAKES ABOUT 3 CUPS (750 ML) ◆ 9 TO 12 ICE POPS

Strawberries are versatile fruits that readily embrace many added flavors,
but when fresh berries are at their peak, they need little help to shine.
You can use thawed frozen strawberries here.

Blender

4 cups (1 L) chopped hulled strawberries

1/2 cup (125 mL) water

1/4 cup (60 mL) brown rice syrup or 3 tbsp (45 mL) agave or corn syrup

3 tbsp (45 mL) extra-fine (fruit) sugar or granulated sugar

2 tbsp (30 mL) freshly squeezed lemon juice

1 In blender at medium speed, purée strawberries, water, syrup, sugar and lemon juice, ensuring that sugar is fully dissolved. Pass through a fine-mesh sieve, if desired (see Tip, below).

2 Pour into molds and freeze until slushy, then insert sticks and freeze until solid, for at least 4 hours. If you are using an ice pop kit, follow the manufacturer's instructions.

Tip

I prefer to strain the fine seeds out of the mix before freezing.

Raspberry
Ice Pops

MAKES ABOUT 2²/₃ CUPS (650 ML) ◆ **8 TO 10 ICE POPS**

An intensely flavored apple juice made from frozen concentrate
sweetens naturally tart raspberries without sugar or syrup.

Fine-mesh sieve

3 cups (750 mL) fresh or frozen
raspberries

1 cup (250 mL) water

¹/₂ cup (125 mL) frozen unsweetened
apple juice concentrate

1 In a saucepan, combine raspberries, water and
concentrate. Bring to a simmer and cook until fruit is
very soft, 2 to 5 minutes. Strain through sieve placed
over a large measuring cup, pressing down on solids
to extract as much pulp and juice as possible. Discard
solids. Set aside to cool.

2 Pour into molds and freeze until slushy, then insert
sticks and freeze until solid, for at least 4 hours. If you
are using an ice pop kit, follow the manufacturer's
instructions.

Cranberry
Ice Pops

MAKES ABOUT 2²/₃ CUPS (650 ML) ◆ 8 TO 10 ICE POPS

This is an ice pop for true cranberry lovers.

Fine-mesh sieve

3 cups (750 mL) fresh or frozen cranberries

2 cups (500 mL) apple juice or apple cider

1/3 cup (75 mL) granulated sugar

1 tsp (5 mL) finely grated orange zest

1 In a saucepan, combine cranberries, apple juice, sugar and orange zest. Bring to a boil, stirring until sugar is dissolved. Reduce heat and simmer, covered, until berries are falling apart, about 15 minutes for fresh berries and 10 minutes for frozen.

2 Strain through sieve placed over a large measuring cup, pressing down on solids with a rubber spatula to extract as much pulp and juice as possible. Discard solids. Set aside to cool.

3 Pour into molds and freeze until slushy, then insert sticks and freeze until solid, for at least 4 hours. If you are using an ice pop kit, follow the manufacturer's instructions.

Tip

This deep red pop is pleasantly but decidedly on the tart side. If you prefer a sweet ice pop, increase the sugar to 1/2 cup (125 mL).

Wild Blueberry
Ice Pops

MAKES ABOUT 3 CUPS (750 ML) ◆ 9 TO 12 ICE POPS

Wild blueberries are smaller and have a more intense flavor than cultivated varieties. If you don't pick your own or live in a place where fresh wild blueberries are common, frozen ones are easy to find. They are just as good as fresh for these ice pops.

Fine-mesh sieve

3 cups (750 mL) wild blueberries

1 cup (250 mL) water

$1/3$ cup (75 mL) apple juice concentrate

$1/4$ cup (60 mL) light agave, corn syrup or honey, or $1/3$ cup (75 mL) brown rice syrup (see Tip, right)

2 tbsp (30 mL) freshly squeezed lemon juice

1 In a saucepan, combine blueberries, water, apple juice concentrate, syrup and lemon juice. Bring to a boil, then reduce heat and simmer, stirring often, until fruit is falling apart, about 3 minutes for frozen fruit or up to 8 minutes for fresh. Strain through sieve placed over a large measuring cup, pressing down on solids with a rubber spatula to extract as much pulp and juice as possible. Discard solids. Set aside to cool.

2 Pour into molds and freeze until slushy, then insert sticks and freeze until solid, for at least 4 hours. If you are using an ice pop kit, follow the manufacturer's instructions.

Tip

If you have access to blueberry honey, which can be difficult to find, use it to replace the syrup. Blueberry honey has medium body, full flavor and a subtle blueberry aftertaste.

Pomegranate
Ice Pops

MAKES ABOUT 2¹/₄ CUPS (550 ML) ◆ 6 TO 9 ICE POPS

Natural pomegranate juice makes a nice ice pop all by itself,
but it is more palatable if slightly sweetened. Because the pomegranate
flavor is so special, I prefer to use light corn syrup, which has a neutral taste,
as a sweetener, but you can experiment with honey or other syrups.

---

2 cups (500 mL) unsweetened pomegranate juice, divided

3 tbsp (45 mL) corn, agave or brown rice syrup or liquid honey

VARIATIONS

POMEGRANATE WATERMELON ICE POPS:
After mixing pomegranate juice and syrup (Step 1), place in a blender. Add 3 cups (750 mL) chopped seedless watermelon and purée until smooth. Strain through a fine-mesh sieve and complete Step 2. Makes about 4 cups (1 L) or 12 to 16 ice pops.

POMEGRANATE APPLE ICE POPS: Replace syrup with ¹/₂ cup (125 mL) frozen unsweetened apple juice concentrate and ¹/₃ cup (75 mL) water. Makes about 2³/₄ cups (675 mL) or 8 to 11 ice pops.

1 In a microwavable container, mix ¹/₄ cup (60 mL) juice with syrup. Heat until mixture is thin, about 10 to 20 seconds on High. (You can also do this on the stovetop, in a small saucepan over medium heat, heating for about 1 minute.) Stir into remaining juice, mixing well.

2 Pour into molds and freeze until slushy, then insert sticks and freeze until solid, for at least 4 hours. If you are using an ice pop kit, follow the manufacturer's instructions.

Tips

It is more economical — and definitely more convenient — to use bottled 100% pomegranate juice.

If you are making juice from fresh pomegranates, cut the fruit in half and use a grapefruit or orange juicer to extract the juice; one large pomegranate yields about ¹/₂ cup (125 mL) juice. Otherwise, remove the seeds, discarding skin and pulp, and put the seeds through a food mill. You can also put them in a blender and blend briefly, trying not to break up the seed kernels, and strain.

Pomegranate Berry
Ice Pops

MAKES ABOUT 3 CUPS (750 ML) ◆ 9 TO 12 ICE POPS

Pomegranate juice makes a wonderful base for strong-flavored berries such as wild blueberries or raspberries. The result is an intensely fruity, pleasantly tart and undoubtedly healthy ice pop. You can use frozen berries year-round for convenience.

Blender

Fine-mesh sieve

2 cups (500 mL) unsweetened pomegranate juice, divided

3 tbsp (45 mL) agave or corn syrup, or $1/4$ cup (60 mL) brown rice syrup

2 cups (500 mL) wild blueberries, raspberries or blackberries, thawed if frozen

1 In a glass measuring cup, mix $1/4$ cup (60 mL) pomegranate juice with syrup. Heat in a microwave oven until mixture is thin, about 10 to 20 seconds on High. (You can also do this on the stovetop, in a small saucepan over medium heat, heating for about 1 minute.) Add to blender with remaining juice and berries; purée at medium speed (see Tip, below).

2 Strain through sieve placed over a large measuring cup, pressing down and scraping solids with a rubber spatula to extract as much pulp and juice as possible. Discard solids.

3 Pour into molds and freeze until slushy, then insert sticks and freeze until solid, for at least 4 hours. If you are using an ice pop kit, follow the manufacturer's instructions.

Tip

Because every brand of blender has a different power capacity, speeds vary greatly. Generally, to purée a mixture, start at slow to medium speed and move up to medium-high speed on a powerful blender, or high speed on a less powerful model. If the engine is very strong, too much air may be incorporated into the mixture at high speed.

Concord Grape
Ice Pops

MAKES ABOUT 2⅓ CUPS (575 ML) ◆ 7 TO 9 ICE POPS

Native North American grapes are full of rich sweet-and-sour fruity flavors that are considered too "foxy" for fine wine. Fortunately they make wonderful desserts, jams and jellies, as this ice pop proves.

Fine-mesh sieve

1 lb (500 g) Concord (blue) or Coronation grapes (about 3 cups/750 mL)

1 cup (250 mL) water

⅓ cup (75 mL) granulated sugar

1 In a saucepan, combine grapes, water and sugar. Bring to a boil, stirring until sugar is dissolved. Reduce heat and simmer, covered, until grapes are falling apart, about 10 minutes. Over a large measuring cup, strain through sieve, pressing down and scraping solids with a rubber spatula to extract as much pulp and juice as possible. Discard skins and seeds. Set aside to cool.

2 Pour into molds and freeze until slushy, then insert sticks and freeze until solid, for at least 4 hours. If you are using an ice pop kit, follow the manufacturer's instructions.

Tip

Concord grapes (also called blue grapes) and Coronation grapes have very similar flavor profiles, but Coronation grapes are seedless.

Mango
Ice Pops

MAKES ABOUT 3 CUPS (750 ML) ◆ **9 TO 12 ICE POPS**

Using a combination of cooked and fresh mango makes these ice pops
an exceptionally flavorful and honest expression of the fruit.
Make sure you use only fully ripe mangoes.

Blender

2 cups (500 mL) chopped fresh ripe mango, divided

$1^1/_4$ cups (300 mL) water, divided

$^1/_3$ cup (75 mL) granulated sugar

2 tbsp (30 mL) freshly squeezed lime juice

1 In a saucepan, combine $^2/_3$ cup (150 mL) mango, $^3/_4$ cup (175 mL) water and sugar. Bring to a boil, stirring until sugar is dissolved. Reduce heat and simmer, uncovered, for 5 minutes. Set aside to cool.

2 In blender, at medium-high speed, purée cooked mango mixture, remaining $1^1/_3$ cups (325 mL) mango, $^1/_2$ cup (125 mL) water and lime juice.

3 Pour into molds and freeze until slushy, then insert sticks and freeze until solid, for at least 4 hours. If you are using an ice pop kit, follow the manufacturer's instructions.

Tip

A ripe mango should be fragrant, and soft but not mushy to the touch. If you see sap oozing from the stem end, it's a good sign that the mango is sweet and ripe.

Pure Pineapple
Ice Pops

MAKES ABOUT 3$^1/_2$ CUPS (875 ML) ◆ **10 TO 14 ICE POPS**

Choose a perfectly ripe pineapple for these delicious ice pops. They are made from cooked pineapple, which gives them a mellow yet full flavor.

---

1 pineapple, peeled, cored and minced (see Tip, right)

2$^1/_2$ cups (625 mL) water

Pinch salt

$^2/_3$ cup (150 mL) granulated sugar

1 In a saucepan over high heat, bring pineapple, with juices, water and salt to a boil. Reduce heat to medium and boil for 10 minutes. Add sugar and stir until dissolved, then reduce heat and simmer for 5 minutes. Remove from heat and set aside to cool.

2 Pour into molds and freeze until slushy, then insert sticks and freeze until solid, for at least 4 hours. If you are using an ice pop kit, follow the manufacturer's instructions.

Tip

To mince pineapple: Peel pineapple, removing eyes. Cut in half lengthwise, then cut each half lengthwise into 4 pieces. Cut out core. Thinly slice each piece lengthwise, then stack pieces and slice crosswise into a thin julienne. Cut across julienne to mince. Save the juices on the cutting board for use in the recipe.

Pineapple Sage
Ice Pops

MAKES ABOUT 3¹/₃ CUPS (825 ML) ◆ **10 TO 13 ICE POPS**

Sweet ripe, fresh pineapple plus a subtle undertone
of sage makes a fantastic flavor combination.

Blender or food processor

1¹/₃ cups (325 mL) water

³/₄ cup (175 mL) granulated sugar

12 fresh sage leaves

¹/₄ tsp (1 mL) salt

1 pineapple, peeled

1 In a saucepan, combine water, sugar, sage and salt. Bring to a boil, stirring until sugar is dissolved, then reduce heat and simmer for 1 minute. Remove from heat and set aside to cool. Remove and discard sage leaves.

2 Cut pineapple lengthwise into quarters and cut out and discard core. Roughly chop two of the quarters and place in blender with sage syrup. Purée. Chop remaining pineapple, add to mixture and pulse just until pineapple is crushed (finer than minced but not puréed).

3 Pour into molds and freeze until slushy, then insert sticks and freeze until solid, for at least 4 hours. If you are using an ice pop kit, follow the manufacturer's instructions.

Tip

Because every brand of blender has a different power capacity, speeds vary greatly. Generally, to purée a mixture, start at slow to medium speed and move up to medium-high speed, on a powerful blender, or high speed, on a less powerful model. If the engine is very strong, too much air may be incorporated into the mixture at high speed.

Lychee
Ice Pops

For lychee ice pops, readily available canned lychees, surprisingly,
give just as good results as fresh lychees, which have a short season
and are much more expensive and fussier to prepare.

Blender

Fine-mesh sieve

2 cans (each 20 oz/565 g) lychees,
drained, syrup reserved

1 tsp (5 mL) grated lime zest

$1/3$ cup + 1 tbsp (90 mL) freshly
squeezed lime juice

VARIATION
LYCHEE ROSE ICE POPS:
Add 2 tsp (10 mL) rose water
to the lychee mixture before
puréeing.

---

1 In blender, at medium-high speed, purée lychees,
$1^1/3$ cups (325 mL) reserved lychee syrup, and lime
zest and juice. Discard remaining lychee syrup. Strain
purée through sieve placed over a large measuring cup,
pushing down on solids with a rubber spatula to extract
as much pulp and juice as possible. Discard solids.

2 Pour into molds and freeze until slushy, then insert
sticks and freeze until solid, for at least 4 hours. If you
are using an ice pop kit, follow the manufacturer's
instructions.

Tip
Always use freshly squeezed lemon juice or lime juice
in your ice pops; bottled just doesn't compare.

Coconut
Ice Pops

MAKES ABOUT 2$\frac{1}{4}$ CUPS (550 ML) ◆ 6 TO 9 ICE POPS

Coconut milk — the juice extracted from grated mature coconut flesh mixed with water — has a natural affinity with palm sugar, which is made from the sweet sap of various palm trees. These two ingredients are all you need to make a perfect tropical ice pop.

$\frac{1}{2}$ cup (125 mL) palm sugar (see Tips, right)

3 tbsp (45 mL) water

2 cups (500 mL) coconut milk (see Tips, right)

1 In a saucepan over medium-low heat, melt sugar in water, stirring until smooth. Stir in coconut milk; increase heat to high and bring to a boil, stirring. Reduce heat to medium-low and simmer for 1 minute. Set aside to cool.

2 Pour into molds and freeze until slushy, then insert sticks and freeze until solid, for at least 4 hours. If you are using an ice pop kit, follow the manufacturer's instructions.

VARIATIONS

CARDAMOM-SCENTED COCONUT ICE POPS:
After the sugar is melted, stir in 4 crushed cardamom pods or $\frac{1}{4}$ tsp (1 mL) ground cardamom before adding the coconut milk. When cool, strain out the spice.

VANILLA COCONUT ICE POPS: Stir $\frac{1}{2}$ tsp (2 mL) vanilla extract to cooled coconut mixture.

PANDAN LEAF–SCENTED COCONUT ICE POPS:
Add 1 pandan (pandanus) leaf to the coconut mixture before bringing it to a boil (double leaf over lengthwise and tie it in a knot). Simmer and let steep, covered, for 10 minutes. Remove leaf and set aside to cool.

Tips

Palm sugar is used extensively in Asian cooking and is generally available at Asian food stores and at many other supermarkets. It is usually sold in solid tablets or cakes measuring about $\frac{1}{4}$ cup (60 mL) each; chop or grate the cakes into loose sugar before measuring. "Coconut sugar," which is palm sugar made from coconut sap, is sold in granulated form at bulk and natural foods stores.

You can substitute an equal quantity of light brown (golden yellow) sugar or raw cane sugar for the palm sugar.

Papaya Milkshake
Ice Pops

MAKES ABOUT 2³/₄ CUPS (675 ML) ◆ 8 TO 11 ICE POPS

Papaya milkshakes are extremely popular throughout tropical Asia, and they make great ice pops too. Even better, they are simple to make.

Blender

1¹/₂ cups (375 mL) chopped fresh papaya

1 cup (250 mL) milk

2 tbsp (30 mL) extra-fine (fruit) sugar or granulated sugar

2 tbsp (30 mL) liquid honey

1 In blender at medium-high speed, purée papaya, milk, sugar and honey, ensuring that sugar is fully dissolved.

2 Pour into molds and freeze until slushy, then insert sticks and freeze until solid, for at least 4 hours. If you are using an ice pop kit, follow the manufacturer's instructions.

Tips

A ripe papaya should be fairly soft and give when gently pressed, but it shouldn't be mushy. Halve the papaya and spoon out the seeds, then use the spoon to scoop out its tender flesh. Avoid spooning out any of the harder, less ripe flesh closer to the skin.

Extra-fine sugar (fruit sugar) is just granulated sugar with extremely small crystals, which dissolve quickly in cold or thick liquids. It's useful for sweetening fruit purées or mixtures that are uncooked or cold. You can make your own by grinding regular granulated sugar in a blender.

Banana
Ice Pops

MAKES ABOUT 3 CUPS (750 ML) ◆ 9 TO 12 ICE POPS

Use ripe, sweet bananas for these ice pops, which can be made in the blink of an eye. The touch of molasses adds a lot to these treats — use whatever type you have on hand.

Blender

$2^1/_2$ cups (625 mL) sliced ripe bananas (3 medium-large)

$2/_3$ cup (150 mL) 5% (light) cream, whole milk or evaporated milk

$1/_2$ cup (125 mL) water

3 tbsp (45 mL) brown rice, agave or corn syrup

1 tsp (5 mL) molasses

1 In blender at medium-high speed, purée bananas, cream, water, syrup and molasses.

2 Pour into molds and freeze until slushy, then insert sticks and freeze until solid, for at least 4 hours. If you are using an ice pop kit, follow the manufacturer's instructions.

Tip

You can vary the flavor by using different varieties of bananas. Red-skinned bananas and mini-bananas are particularly good for sweet preparations such as these pops.

VARIATION

BANANA AND HONEY ICE POPS: Replace the syrup with the same amount of buckwheat honey or other rich, dark liquid honey (such as manuka or avocado). Omit the molasses.

Rhubarb Mint
Ice Pops

MAKES ABOUT 2$^1/_2$ CUPS (625 ML) ◆ 7 TO 10 ICE POPS

Tart rhubarb and sweet mint make a smooth pair in these pretty pink ice pops. The flavor is piqued by just a hint of black pepper.

Fine-mesh sieve

1 lb (500 g) rhubarb, sliced (about 3$^1/_2$ cups/875 mL)

2 cups (500 mL) water

$^2/_3$ cup (150 mL) granulated sugar

4 strips lemon zest, $^1/_2$ by 2 inches (1 by 5 cm) each

4 black peppercorns, bruised (see Tip, right)

1 cup (250 mL) lightly packed fresh mint leaves

1 In a saucepan, combine rhubarb, water, sugar, lemon zest and peppercorns. Bring to a boil, reduce heat and simmer, covered, for 15 minutes. Remove from heat and stir in mint. Cover and set aside to steep for 10 minutes.

2 Place sieve over a large measuring cup and strain, pressing down on solids to extract as much juice as possible. Discard solids.

3 Pour into molds and freeze until slushy, then insert sticks and freeze until solid, for at least 4 hours. If you are using an ice pop kit, follow the manufacturer's instructions.

Tip

Bruise peppercorns by pressing down on them and rolling with the side of a chef's knife or the bottom of a heavy saucepan. You want to crush or crack them a bit, not grind them into powder.

Honeydew Jalapeño
Ice Pops

MAKES ABOUT 3 CUPS (750 ML) ◆ **9 TO 12 ICE POPS**

Lightly sweet and slightly hot, these intriguing ice pops are very refreshing.
Try serving them between savory courses at a barbecue or casual summer dinner.

Blender

$1/3$ cup (75 mL) granulated sugar

$1/3$ cup (75 mL) water

1 jalapeño pepper, seeded and minced

2 strips lime zest, about $1/2$ by 2 inches (1 by 5 cm) each

4 cups (1 L) chopped honeydew melon

3 tbsp (45 mL) freshly squeezed lime juice

1 tbsp (15 mL) chopped fresh cilantro leaves

Pinch salt

1 In a small saucepan, combine sugar, water, jalapeño and lime zest. Bring to a boil, reduce heat and simmer for 1 minute. Remove from heat, cover and set aside to steep for 5 minutes. Remove and discard zest.

2 In blender at medium-high speed, purée melon, lime juice, cilantro and a scant pinch salt. Add reserved jalapeño syrup and blend at low speed just until integrated.

3 Pour into molds and freeze until slushy, then insert sticks and freeze until solid, for at least 4 hours. If you are using an ice pop kit, follow the manufacturer's instructions.

Tip

In many ice pops that include solid ingredients or combine liquids of different viscosities, there is a bit of layering after freezing, which is normal. However, if you want a seamless result, give the mixture a stir after it has reached the slushy stage to ensure the ingredients remain integrated.

Lemon Honey Mint
Ice Pops

MAKES ABOUT 3¹/₂ CUPS (875 ML) ◆ 10 TO 14 ICE POPS

Soothing and sweet, fragrant and tart, this lemony ice pop
is as refreshing as it is delicious.

Fine-mesh sieve

2¹/₂ cups (625 mL) water

1 cup (250 mL) lightly packed fresh mint leaves

Zest of 2 lemons, cut into strips (see Tips, right)

¹/₂ cup (125 mL) liquid honey (see Tips, right)

²/₃ cup (150 mL) freshly squeezed lemon juice

1 In a saucepan, bring water to a boil; remove from heat and add mint and lemon zest. Cover and set aside to steep for 10 minutes.

2 Place sieve over a large measuring cup and strain infusion. Discard solids. Stir in honey until fully incorporated. Stir in lemon juice.

3 Pour into molds and freeze until slushy, then insert sticks and freeze until solid, for at least 4 hours. If you are using an ice pop kit, follow the manufacturer's instructions.

Tips

Because Meyer lemons have exceptionally fragrant zest, they are ideal for these ice pops.

Use a light honey such as orange blossom, alfalfa, clover, wildflower or acacia.

> **VARIATIONS**
>
> **LEMON BALM HONEY ICE POPS:** Replace the mint with ²/₃ cup (150 mL) lightly packed lemon balm leaves.
>
> **LEMON VERBENA HONEY ICE POPS:** Replace the mint with ²/₃ cup (150 mL) lightly packed lemon verbena leaves.

Watermelon Chile
Ice Pops

MAKES ABOUT 3 CUPS (750 ML) ◆ 9 TO 12 ICE POPS

Red-hot peppers flavor the syrup for these unusual ice pops,
which, despite the touch of heat, are still very refreshing.

Blender

Fine-mesh sieve

$1/3$ cup (75 mL) granulated sugar

$1/3$ cup (75 mL) water

2 tbsp (30 mL) minced seeded
red finger chile peppers

Pinch salt

4 cups (1 L) chopped seedless
(or seeded) watermelon

2 tbsp (30 mL) freshly squeezed
lemon juice

1 In a small saucepan, combine sugar, water, chile peppers and salt. Bring to a boil, reduce heat and simmer for 2 minutes. Remove from heat and set aside to cool.

2 In blender at medium-high speed, blend watermelon and lemon juice until smooth. Place sieve over a large measuring cup and strain mixture, pressing down on solids to extract as much pulp and juice as possible. Discard solids. Return mixture to blender and add reserved chile syrup. Blend until chiles are reduced to tiny specks.

3 Pour into molds and freeze until slushy, then insert sticks and freeze until solid, for at least 4 hours. If you are using an ice pop kit, follow the manufacturer's instructions.

Tip

Although the recipe calls for seedless watermelon for convenience, it is still a good idea to strain the mixture, to remove any soft white immature seeds that dot the flesh.

Creamy, Carbonated & Caffeinated

Caramel
Ice Pops

MAKES ABOUT 3²/₃ CUPS (900 ML) ◆ 11 TO 14 ICE POPS

These ice pops are sweet and creamy, with a strong caramel flavor. The high sugar content prevents them from freezing hard, but they are certainly stable enough to enjoy if you let them freeze overnight. Just don't keep them out of the freezer for too long before serving (definitely not the ice pop for a picnic on a hot summer day!).

---

1 cup (250 mL) granulated sugar

Pinch sea salt

2 cups (500 mL) water, divided

2 tbsp (30 mL) butter

³/₄ cup (175 mL) evaporated milk

1 In a heavy-bottomed saucepan, combine sugar, salt and ¹/₂ cup (125 mL) water. Over high heat, bring to a boil and cook, without stirring, until sugar is melted and turns a warm, deep, nutty brown.

2 Remove from heat. Turning head away and standing well back (mixture will sputter), stir in butter and remaining 1¹/₂ cups (375 mL) water. Return to medium heat and cook, stirring, until mixture is smooth and no longer bubbling. Remove from heat and stir in evaporated milk. Set aside to cool.

3 Pour into molds and freeze until slushy, then insert sticks and freeze until solid, for at least 12 hours. If you are using an ice pop kit, follow the manufacturer's instructions.

Tip

If sugar crystallizes on the side of the saucepan while you are caramelizing it (Step 1), soak a pastry brush in water and use it to brush down any crystals.

Fudge
Ice Pops

MAKES ABOUT 3 CUPS (750 ML) ◆ 9 TO 12 ICE POPS

These ice pops are rich and chocolate-fudgy, definitely a step up from the commercial treat, but they still retain the youthful spirit of a fun indulgence.

$2^1/_4$ cups (550 mL) milk

1 tbsp (15 mL) tapioca flour
(see Tips, right)

$^1/_2$ cup (125 mL) unsweetened cocoa powder

2 oz (60 g) semisweet chocolate, chopped

$^3/_4$ cup (175 mL) sweetened condensed milk

$^3/_4$ tsp (3 mL) vanilla extract

1 In a saucepan, whisk together milk and tapioca flour, then whisk in cocoa. Whisking constantly, bring to a boil; reduce heat and simmer, stirring often, for 5 minutes. Remove from heat and whisk in chocolate, until melted, thoroughly incorporated and smooth. Stir in condensed milk and vanilla. Set aside to cool.

2 Pour into molds and freeze until slushy, then insert sticks and freeze until solid, for at least 4 hours. If you are using an ice pop kit, follow the manufacturer's instructions.

Tip

Tapioca flour is often called tapioca starch. They are identical products.

Hazelnut Chocolate
Ice Pops

MAKES ABOUT 2$^1/_2$ CUPS (625 ML) ◆ 7 TO 10 ICE POPS

If you love truffles and other chocolates with nut and nut cream fillings, you'll be a fan of these ice pops, which are nutty and chocolaty without being overwhelmingly rich.

Blender

Fine-mesh sieve

1 cup (250 mL) roasted hazelnuts (see Tip, right)

1$^3/_4$ cups (425 mL) water

$^1/_3$ cup + 2 tbsp (105 mL) granulated sugar

$^2/_3$ cup (150 mL) evaporated milk

1$^3/_4$ oz (50 g) bittersweet or semisweet chocolate, chopped

1 In a saucepan over medium heat, combine hazelnuts, water and sugar; bring to a simmer. Cover, reduce heat to low and simmer for 1 hour. Remove from heat and set aside to cool.

2 Transfer to blender and blend at medium speed until mixture forms a paste. Add evaporated milk and blend at medium speed for 1 minute, then at high speed for 1 or 2 minutes, until mixture is as smooth as possible. Strain through sieve into a saucepan, discarding solids. Bring to a simmer over low heat; simmer, stirring constantly, for 2 minutes. Remove from heat and whisk in chocolate, until thoroughly incorporated and smooth. Set aside to cool.

3 Pour into molds and freeze until slushy, then insert sticks and freeze until solid, for at least 4 hours. If you are using an ice pop kit, follow the manufacturer's instructions.

Tip

You can buy already roasted hazelnuts (rub as much skin off the nuts as possible) or you can make your own. Roast in a 350°F (180°C) oven for about 10 minutes (check after 8 minutes) or toast in a dry skillet over medium heat, stirring occasionally, for about 7 minutes. Remove most of the skins by rubbing hot nuts in a kitchen towel.

Chocolate Milkshake
Ice Pops

This chocolate ice pop brings back memories of drugstore,
road-stop and ice cream parlor milkshakes.

Blender

2 cups (500 mL) half-and-half (10%) cream

$1/2$ cup (125 mL) sweetened condensed milk

$1/3$ cup + 1 tbsp (90 mL) chocolate syrup

1 tsp (5 mL) vanilla extract

1 In blender at medium-high speed, blend cream, condensed milk, chocolate syrup and vanilla until frothy.

2 Pour into molds and freeze until slushy, then insert sticks and freeze until solid, for at least 4 hours. If you are using an ice pop kit, follow the manufacturer's instructions.

Honey, Yogurt and Pistachio
Ice Pops

MAKES ABOUT 3 CUPS (750 ML) ◆ **9 TO 12 ICE POPS**

Inspired by eastern Mediterranean and Middle Eastern flavors, these ice pops are a refreshing combination of sweet honey, tart yogurt and nutty pistachios. Rose water or orange-flower water adds a light floral note.

4 tsp (20 mL) butter

1/2 cup (125 mL) coarsely chopped raw (unsalted) pistachios

2 tbsp (30 mL) granulated sugar

2 cups (500 mL) plain yogurt (2% to full-fat)

1/2 cup (125 mL) liquid honey

1/2 tsp (2 mL) rose water or orange-flower water

1 In a small skillet over medium heat, melt butter. Add pistachios and stir to coat. Sprinkle with sugar; continue cooking and stirring until sugar is melted, no longer granular and lightly caramelized. Scrape onto a plate and set aside to cool.

2 In a large measuring cup, whisk together yogurt, honey and rose water. Fold in reserved pistachios.

3 Pour into molds and freeze until slushy, then insert sticks and freeze until solid, for at least 4 hours. If you are using an ice pop kit, follow the manufacturer's instructions.

Tip

Because of the large volume of honey used here, its flavor will come through quite strongly. That means your choice of honey will change the taste of the ice pop. If you are using orange-flower water, orange blossom honey is a natural choice to further emphasize the citrus flavor. Other honeys have their own characteristics, which makes it satisfying and fun to vary your choices when cooking.

Maple Walnut
Ice Pops

MAKES ABOUT 2¹/₄ CUPS (550 ML) ◆ 6 TO 9 ICE POPS

The classic North American ice cream pairing of maple flavoring
with walnuts also proves irresistible in ice pop form.

Blender or immersion blender

1 cup (250 mL) walnut halves

1 cup less 2 tbsp (220 mL) water

²/₃ cup (150 mL) maple syrup

1 cup (250 mL) evaporated milk

1 In a dry skillet over medium heat, toast walnuts, turning occasionally, until lightly toasted and fragrant, 6 to 8 minutes. Remove from heat and set aside to cool. Chop finely.

2 In a saucepan, combine chopped walnuts, water and maple syrup. Bring to a boil, reduce heat and simmer, uncovered, for 5 minutes. Remove from heat and set aside to cool for 10 minutes. Add evaporated milk. Transfer to blender and blend at medium-high speed until smooth.

3 Pour into molds and freeze until slushy, then insert sticks and freeze until solid, for at least 4 hours. If you are using an ice pop kit, follow the manufacturer's instructions.

Tip

In this recipe — and almost always when cooking with maple syrup — medium (amber) or dark maple syrups are preferable to the lighter versions, as they have a more robust and richer taste that stands up well to other flavorings. Medium-grade (amber) is an all-purpose maple syrup, while dark is usually reserved for baking and commercial preparations. Light or "fancy" maple syrup is best used as a table syrup.

Toasted Almond
Ice Pops

MAKES ABOUT 2$^1/_3$ CUPS (575 ML) ◆ 7 TO 9 ICE POPS

Almond milk makes a naturally good base for almond ice pops such as these sweet and nutty ones.

$^1/_2$ cup (125 mL) sliced almonds

$^1/_2$ cup (125 mL) packed dark brown sugar

2 tbsp (30 mL) butter or almond oil

Pinch salt

2 cups (500 mL) plain almond milk

$^1/_4$ tsp (1 mL) almond extract

1 In a dry skillet over medium heat, toast almonds, stirring frequently, until fragrant and lightly toasted, 3 to 5 minutes. Remove from heat and set aside.

2 In a saucepan over medium heat, combine brown sugar and butter. Cook, stirring, until sugar is no longer granular but fudgy and forms a loose mass when stirred, 5 to 7 minutes. Stir in reserved toasted almonds and cook for 1 minute. Stir in almond milk and bring to a boil. Remove from heat and set aside to cool. Stir in almond extract.

3 Pour into molds and freeze until slushy, then insert sticks and freeze until solid, for at least 4 hours. If you are using an ice pop kit, follow the manufacturer's instructions.

Creamy Molasses Pecan

Ice Pops

MAKES ABOUT 3 CUPS (750 ML) ◆ 9 TO 12 ICE POPS

A touch of molasses adds a lot of umami to the buttermilk base of these nutty ice pops, which are inspired by the flavors of the American South.

1 tbsp (15 mL) butter

$1/2$ cup (125 mL) chopped pecans

3 tbsp (45 mL) dark brown sugar

$1/4$ tsp (1 mL) nutmeg

Pinch cayenne pepper

$1^1/2$ cups (375 mL) buttermilk

$1/3$ cup + 1 tbsp (90 mL) heavy or whipping (35%) cream

$1/3$ cup + 1 tbsp (90 mL) sweetened condensed milk

3 tbsp (45 mL) light (fancy) molasses

1 In a skillet over medium heat, melt butter; add pecans and stir to coat. Sprinkle with brown sugar, nutmeg and cayenne; continue cooking and stirring until sugar is melted, no longer granular and lightly caramelized. Scrape onto a plate and set aside to cool.

2 Whisk together buttermilk, cream, condensed milk and molasses. Pour into molds, filling three-quarters full. Freeze until slushy. Divide sugared pecans evenly among molds and stir into half-frozen mixture to distribute evenly. Insert sticks and freeze until solid, at least 4 hours in total. If you are using an ice pop kit, follow the manufacturer's instructions.

Lemon Cola
Ice Pops

MAKES ABOUT 2¹/₂ CUPS (625 ML) ◆ 7 TO 10 ICE POPS

In Hong Kong's hot, steamy summer weather, "lemon cola" — iced cola enriched with a generous amount of lemon juice — is a favorite beverage.

2 cans (12 oz/355 mL each) cola

Zest of ¹/₂ lemon, cut into strips

¹/₃ cup (75 mL) freshly squeezed lemon juice

1 In a saucepan, bring cola and lemon zest to a boil. Boil over medium-high heat until reduced by about one-quarter, about 10 minutes. Remove from heat and set aside to cool. Remove and discard zest. Stir in lemon juice.

2 Pour into molds and freeze until slushy, then insert sticks and freeze until solid, for at least 4 hours. If you are using an ice pop kit, follow the manufacturer's instructions.

Root Beer Float
Ice Pops

MAKES ABOUT 2^1/$_2$ CUPS (625 ML) ◆ 7 TO 10 ICE POPS

This is the essence of a perennial favorite, root beer topped with vanilla ice cream.
You can also make it with birch beer, sarsaparilla or cola.

^{1}/$_2$ cup (125 mL) heavy or whipping (35%) cream

2 tbsp (30 mL) sweetened condensed milk

^{1}/$_2$ tsp (2 mL) vanilla extract

1^1/$_2$ cups (375 mL) root beer (see Tip, right)

1 In a large measuring cup, whisk together cream, condensed milk and vanilla. Stir in root beer. After bubbles subside, stir again.

2 Pour into molds, leaving a generous ^{3}/$_4$-inch (2 cm) headspace for bubbling up, and freeze until slushy, then insert sticks and freeze until solid, for at least 4 hours. If you are using an ice pop kit, follow the manufacturer's instructions.

Tip

Many of the root beers made by smaller, craft-style soda pop manufacturers have a much richer flavor than the more common international brands. They are often all-natural or organic.

Peanut Butter and Banana
Ice Pops

MAKES ABOUT 2$\frac{1}{4}$ CUPS (550 ML) ◆ 6 TO 9 ICE POPS

Fans of peanut butter and banana sandwiches will be more than pleased with this easy-to-make ice pop.

Blender

2 ripe bananas, sliced

$\frac{1}{2}$ cup (125 mL) smooth peanut butter

$\frac{1}{2}$ cup (125 mL) water

$\frac{1}{4}$ cup (60 mL) sweetened condensed milk

Pinch salt

1 In blender at medium-high speed, purée bananas, peanut butter, water, condensed milk and salt.

2 Pour into molds and freeze until slushy, then insert sticks and freeze until solid, for at least 4 hours. If you are using an ice pop kit, follow the manufacturer's instructions.

Tips

You can use natural (peanuts only) or prepared peanut butter in these recipes. If using natural peanut butter you may want to add salt and/or sugar to taste.

Thanksgiving Pumpkin Pie
Ice Pops

MAKES ABOUT 3 CUPS (750 ML) ◆ 9 TO 12 ICE POPS

A well-spiced sweet pumpkin pie really summons up images of autumn.
These ice pops capture the delectable flavors of that traditional Thanksgiving treat.

Fine-mesh sieve

1 can (12 oz/170 mL) evaporated milk

1 tsp (5 mL) tapioca flour
(see Tips, page 92)

1$^1/_2$ cups (375 mL) pumpkin or
squash purée (see Tips, right)

$^1/_3$ cup + 2 tbsp (105 mL) granulated
sugar

3 tbsp (45 mL) light (fancy) molasses
or maple syrup

$^1/_2$ tsp (2 mL) ground ginger

$^1/_4$ tsp (1 mL) cinnamon

Pinch nutmeg

Pinch cloves

Pinch white pepper

Pinch salt

2 egg yolks

3 tbsp (45 mL) heavy or whipping
(35%) cream

1 In a saucepan, whisk together evaporated milk and tapioca flour. Whisk in pumpkin purée, sugar, molasses, ginger, cinnamon, a generous pinch of nutmeg, cloves, white pepper and salt. Bring to a boil, stirring constantly. Reduce heat, cover and simmer, stirring often, for 10 minutes. Remove from heat.

2 In a bowl, whisk egg yolks with cream. Add $^1/_4$ cup (60 mL) hot pumpkin mixture and whisk until blended. Whisk into pumpkin mixture in saucepan and place over low heat. Cook, without simmering, and stirring constantly, until steaming hot, 1 to 2 minutes.

Tips

If you prefer, substitute an equal quantity of table (18%) cream, half-and-half (10%) cream or milk for the heavy or whipping (35%) cream.

To make homemade pumpkin or squash purée: Cut vegetable in half lengthwise and remove seeds. Place halves, cut side down, on a rimmed baking sheet. Bake in 425°F (220°C) oven until very tender, 30 to 60 minutes. Remove from oven and set aside to cool. Scoop out flesh and mash well or purée in a food processor.

Espresso
Ice Pops

These ice pops are rather serious — definitely for the dedicated black coffee drinker. They are black, lightly sweetened and deliver a good caffeine punch. Use a dark-roast espresso coffee.

^{1}/$_3$ cup (75 mL) granulated sugar
^{1}/$_3$ cup (75 mL) water
Zest of 1 lemon, cut into strips
2 cups (500 mL) hot espresso or strong black coffee

1 In a small saucepan, bring sugar, water and lemon zest to a boil, stirring until sugar is dissolved. Reduce heat and simmer for 2 minutes. Stir into coffee. Remove from heat and set aside to cool.

2 Strain out and discard zest. Pour into molds and freeze until slushy, then insert sticks and freeze until solid, for at least 4 hours. If you are using an ice pop kit, follow the manufacturer's instructions.

Global

Avocado
Ice Pops

MAKES ABOUT 2 CUPS (500 ML) ◆ 6 TO 8 ICE POPS

In Mexico and other parts of Central America, avocados are sometimes used in sweets. This use certainly won't seem strange to the Filipino, Vietnamese and Indonesian communities, who primarily enjoy the fruit over shaved ice with sweetened condensed milk or in milkshakes. Native to Central America, avocados are one of many examples — including hot peppers, soursops, potatoes, jicama, squash and many legumes — of how Mexican culinary culture spread to Asia through the important Acapulco–Manila clipper-ship trade route from the mid-16th to early 19th centuries.

Blender

1 cup (250 mL) chopped ripe avocado

1/3 cup (75 mL) sweetened condensed milk

3 tbsp (45 mL) freshly squeezed lime juice

Pinch salt

2/3 cup (150 mL) water

3 tbsp (45 mL) extra-fine (fruit) sugar or granulated sugar

1 Place avocado, condensed milk, lime juice and a scant pinch of salt in blender. Stir together water and sugar until sugar is dissolved; add to blender. Purée at medium-high speed.

2 Pour into molds, tapping them on work surface to remove any air pockets. Insert sticks and freeze until solid, for at least 4 hours. If you are using an ice pop kit, follow the manufacturer's instructions.

Caribbean Fruit Punch
Ice Pops

MAKES ABOUT 3¹/₄ CUPS (800 ML) ◆ 9 TO 13 ICE POPS

A typical Caribbean punch is a spirited mix of fruit and flavorings, often accented with a dash of angostura bitters, which is a Trinidadian trick.

Blender

1 cup (250 mL) coconut milk

¹/₃ cup (75 mL) packed dark brown sugar

¹/₂ tsp (2 mL) finely grated lime zest

¹/₄ tsp (1 mL) ground cardamom

¹/₄ tsp (1 mL) freshly grated nutmeg

1¹/₂ cups (375 mL) chopped ripe mango

³/₄ cup (175 mL) sliced banana

¹/₄ cup (60 mL) freshly squeezed lime juice

¹/₂ tsp (2 mL) rum extract

Dash angostura bitters

1 In a saucepan, combine coconut milk, sugar, lime zest, cardamom and a scant ¹/₄ tsp (1 mL) nutmeg. Cook over medium heat until simmering, stirring until sugar is dissolved. Remove from heat and set aside to cool.

2 In blender at medium-high speed, purée mango, banana, lime juice, rum extract, bitters and coconut milk mixture.

3 Pour into molds and freeze until slushy, then insert sticks and freeze until solid, for at least 4 hours. If you are using an ice pop kit, follow the manufacturer's instructions.

Tip

If you have only whole cardamom in pods rather than ground cardamom, crack about 4 pods to obtain ¹/₄ tsp (1 mL) seeds; grind in a mortar before adding to the recipe.

VARIATION

CARIBBEAN RUM PUNCH ICE POPS: Substitute 2 tbsp (30 mL) dark rum for the rum extract, just for the flavor, or up to ¹/₃ cup (75 mL) dark or amber rum to add a bit of a kick. Freeze overnight.

Cucumber Chile
Ice Pops

MAKES ABOUT 3 CUPS (750 ML) ◆ 9 TO 12 ICE POPS

A light touch of dried hot pepper bumps a refreshing cucumber and lime ice pop into a higher realm. This is a delicious traditional Mexican treat.

Fine-mesh sieve

Blender

1 dried guajillo chile pepper

$1/4$ cup (60 mL) granulated sugar

$1/2$ cup (125 mL) water, divided

2 field cucumbers (peel and seeds included), chopped

$1/3$ cup (75 mL) freshly squeezed lime juice

VARIATION

CUCUMBER CHILE COCKTAIL ICE POPS: Stir in 3 tbsp (45 mL) tequila along with the syrup. Gold or reposado tequila will give more flavor, while white tequila will add just a subtle touch of tequila's unique taste.

1 In a small saucepan over medium heat, toast chile pepper, turning occasionally, until lightly darkened and fragrant. Remove from heat and set aside to cool. When chile is cool enough to handle, split it open and remove and discard seeds and inner membranes. Place in a spice grinder or mortar and grind to a fine powder.

2 In saucepan, combine chile powder with sugar and half the water. Bring to boil, stirring until sugar is dissolved. Remove from heat and set aside to cool.

3 In blender at medium speed, blend cucumber, lime juice and remaining water until it resembles thick juice.

4 Place sieve over a large measuring cup and strain cucumber mixture, pressing down on solids with a rubber spatula to extract as much juice as possible. Discard solids. Stir in reserved chile syrup.

5 Pour into molds and freeze until slushy, then insert sticks and freeze until solid, for at least 4 hours. If you are using an ice pop kit, follow the manufacturer's instructions.

Tip

You can use other mild to medium-hot dried chile peppers in these ice pops. Good medium-hot choices are New Mexico chiles, Mexican puyas (which are slightly hotter than guajillos) or pasillo chiles. Avoid dried serrano, arbol and chipotle peppers, because the smoky flavor of the chipotle and the more intense heat of the other two will not go well with the cucumber.

Korean Pear and Ginger

Ice Pops

Pears in Korea — known as Asian pears in North America — are often poached with whole almonds in ginger-flavored syrup, which is the inspiration for these ice pops.

Spice bag or cheesecloth

Blender

6 slices gingerroot

¹/₂ tsp (2 mL) black peppercorns

¹/₂ stick cinnamon (about 1¹/₂ inches/4 cm)

2 cups (500 mL) water

¹/₃ cup (75 mL) rock (yellow crystal) sugar (see Tip, page 50) or granulated sugar

1¹/₂ lbs (750 g) Korean pears (see Tip, right)

¹/₄ tsp (1 mL) almond extract

1 Place ginger, peppercorns and cinnamon in spice bag or wrap in cheesecloth. In a saucepan, bring water and sugar to a boil, stirring until sugar is dissolved. Add spice bag, reduce heat and simmer, covered, for 5 minutes.

2 Meanwhile, peel and core pear(s) and cut into large chunks.

3 Add chopped pear to saucepan and bring to a boil. Reduce heat, cover and simmer until very tender, 20 to 25 minutes. Remove from heat and set aside to cool.

4 Remove and discard spice bag. Stir in almond extract. Transfer to blender and purée at medium-high speed.

5 Pour into molds and freeze until slushy, then insert sticks and freeze until solid, for at least 4 hours. If you are using an ice pop kit, follow the manufacturer's instructions.

Tip

Korean pears are large, heavy, apple-shaped pears with matte light brown skin. They range in weight from about 12 ounces (375 g) to 1¹/₂ pounds (750 g) each. Like many other Asian varieties, they are often called simply Asian pears, or Japanese, Taiwan or sand pears, so named for the slightly sandy texture of their flesh. Korean pears have a distinctive sweet-and-sour contrast and firm, crisp texture, making them ideal pears for cooking. Don't peel them too far in advance, as they tend to oxidize a little when exposed to air.

Pineapple Coconut
Ice Pops

MAKES ABOUT 3 CUPS (750 ML) ◆ 9 TO 12 ICE POPS

These ice pops, made from fresh pineapple cooked in coconut milk and flavored with toasted coconut, are almost as good as a lazy day on a Mexican beach.

Blender

1/2 cup (125 mL) sweetened flaked coconut

1/2 pineapple, peeled, cored and chopped

1 cup (250 mL) coconut milk

1/3 cup (75 mL) light brown (golden yellow) sugar

Pinch salt

1/4 cup (60 mL) water

VARIATION

PIÑA COLADA ICE POPS: Do not toast coconut (omit Step 1). Replace the water with an equal quantity of white or amber rum.

---

1 In a dry skillet over medium-low heat, toast coconut, stirring often, until golden brown and fragrant, about 5 minutes. Remove from heat and set aside.

2 In a saucepan, combine pineapple, coconut milk, sugar and salt. Bring to a boil, reduce heat and simmer, covered, for 15 minutes. Remove from heat, uncover and set aside to cool.

3 Transfer to blender and add water; blend at medium speed until smooth. Add reserved toasted coconut and blend at low speed just until combined.

4 Pour into molds and freeze until slushy, then insert sticks and freeze until solid, for at least 4 hours. If you are using an ice pop kit, follow the manufacturer's instructions.

Tip

In many ice pops that include solid ingredients or combine liquids of different viscosities, there is a bit of layering after freezing, which is normal. However, if you want a seamless result, give the mixture a stir after it has reached the slushy stage to ensure that the ingredients remain integrated.

Sweet Sesame
Ice Pops

MAKES ABOUT 2³/₄ CUPS (675 ML) ◆ 8 TO 11 ICE POPS

Sesame ice pops made from black sesame seeds are very popular in China. As soon as iced desserts began to become popular there — in the early twentieth century, when electricity became widely available — traditional hot and cold sweet soups were turned into frozen ice pops, or "ice sticks" (bingbang, as they are known in Mandarin).

Blender

1 cup (250 mL) raw black sesame seeds (see Tips, right)

¹/₄ cup (60 mL) blanched skinned peanuts (see Tips, right)

³/₄ cup (175 mL) granulated sugar

2 tbsp (30 mL) sweet rice flour or tapioca flour (see Tips, page 92)

2 cups (500 mL) water

1 In a dry skillet or wok over medium heat, cook sesame seeds, stirring constantly, until fragrant and toasted, about 10 minutes. Scrape onto a plate and set aside to cool.

2 In same pan, toast peanuts, stirring often, until golden and fragrant, about 10 minutes. Scrape onto a plate and set aside to cool.

3 In blender, combine sesame seeds, peanuts and sugar; blend at high speed until finely ground. Add rice flour and pulse to combine thoroughly. Add water and blend until smooth.

4 Scrape sesame mixture into a saucepan and bring to a boil over high heat, stirring constantly. Reduce heat to medium and simmer, stirring constantly, for 3 minutes. Remove from heat and set aside to cool.

5 Spoon into molds. Tap molds on work surface to remove any air bubbles. Insert sticks and freeze until solid, for at least 4 hours. If you are using an ice pop kit, follow the manufacturer's instructions.

Tips

Black sesame seeds are available at all Chinese, Japanese and Korean grocery stores, as well as many supermarkets. For convenience, you can buy already roasted sesame seeds and peanuts and skip Steps 1 and 2 in the recipe. However, if you roast your own seeds and peanuts, the result will be more fragrant.

If you prefer, substitute ¹/₄ cup (60 mL) peanut butter for the peanuts. Skip Step 2 and add along with the water in Step 3.

Cashew
Ice Pops

MAKES ABOUT 2¹/₂ CUPS (625 ML) ◆ 8 TO 10 ICE POPS

Rich, creamy cashew nuts are a favorite ingredient for sweets in tropical Asia, and they shine in these delicious ice pops.

Blender

2 cups (500 mL) whole raw cashew nuts (8¹/₂ oz/265 g, see Tips, right)

³/₄ cup (175 mL) palm sugar, raw cane sugar or light brown (golden yellow) sugar (see Tips, right)

¹/₄ cup (60 mL) water

1 cup (250 mL) evaporated milk or cooled scalded coconut milk (see Tips, right)

1 In a dry, heavy-bottomed skillet over low heat, toast cashews, stirring frequently, until golden, 15 to 18 minutes. Remove from heat and set aside to cool. Chop ¹/₃ cup (75 mL) and transfer to a small bowl. Set aside.

2 In a small saucepan over medium heat, heat sugar and water until sugar dissolves. Remove from heat and set aside to cool.

3 In blender at medium-high speed, purée whole cashews, sugar syrup and evaporated milk until smooth.

4 Pour cashew mixture into molds, leaving a scant ¹/₂ inch (1 cm) headspace. Divide reserved chopped cashews evenly among molds, stirring to distribute evenly. Freeze until slushy, then insert sticks and freeze until solid, for at least 4 hours. If you are using an ice pop kit, follow the manufacturer's instructions.

Tips

For convenience, you can use unsalted roasted cashews instead of toasting your own; they will, however, not be as fragrant as freshly toasted ones.

Each different sugar will provide a unique flavor in these ice pops. Look for raw cane sugar in Asian and Latin American markets, where it is known as piloncillo. Palm sugar, which is produced from the sweet sap of various palm trees, is sold in cakes; it should be chopped before measuring.

For scalded coconut milk, bring coconut milk to a full boil, remove from heat and set aside to cool.

Red Bean
Ice Pops

This was one of the first and is still one of the most popular ice pop recipes in Japan and China.

Food processor

1 cup (250 mL) dried red adzuki beans

Water

$^3/_4$ cup + 2 tbsp (205 mL) granulated sugar

1 cup (250 mL) milk

1 cup (250 mL) half-and-half (10%) cream

VARIATIONS

RED BEAN AND COCONUT ICE POPS: These dairy-free ice pops are popular in the Philippines and Taiwan. Replace the milk and cream with 2 cups (500 mL) scalded coconut milk (see Tip, page 121).

BROWN SUGAR RED BEAN ICE POPS: Replace the granulated sugar with packed brown sugar (demerara, light brown/golden yellow and dark brown are all fine) and 2 tbsp (30 mL) light (fancy) molasses.

---

1 Cover beans with water by 2 inches (5 cm) and soak for at least 4 hours or overnight. Drain, rinse well and place in a saucepan with 2 cups (500 mL) water. Bring to a boil over high heat. Reduce heat to medium and cook until beans are soft, adding a little more water if level gets below top of beans, 25 to 60 minutes (see Tip, below). Stir in sugar until dissolved and cook, stirring often, until liquid is reduced to about 2 tbsp (30 mL), about 15 minutes. Remove from heat.

2 Scoop out $^1/_3$ cup (75 mL) beans and set aside. Transfer remainder to food processor fitted with the metal blade. Add milk and cream and process until smooth. (You can also do this in a blender, or by hand with a potato masher.) Set aside to cool. Stir in reserved whole beans.

3 Pour into molds and freeze until slushy, then insert sticks and freeze until solid, for at least 4 hours. If you are using an ice pop kit, follow the manufacturer's instructions.

Tip

The cooking time for beans depends upon their freshness and how long they were soaked. Older beans will take longer to cook.

Traditional Kulfi
Ice Pops

MAKES ABOUT 3¹/₃ CUPS (825 ML) ◆ 10 TO 13 ICE POPS

This is the traditional way to make kulfi, India's version of ice cream pops: from concentrated milk that has been cooked down to about a third of its volume. As boiling down the milk is a bit time-consuming, many home cooks don't make these ice pops. But they are better than any commercial ones I've tried, so I think they are well worth the effort.

Fine-mesh sieve

7 cups (1.75 L) whole milk

1 cup (250 mL) half-and-half (10%) cream (see Tip, right)

8 cardamom pods, crushed

3 whole cloves

¹/₂ cup (125 mL) granulated sugar

2 tbsp (30 mL) chopped blanched almonds

2 tbsp (30 mL) chopped natural pistachios (skins rubbed off) or blanched almonds

1 In a large, wide, heavy-bottomed saucepan or Dutch oven, combine milk, cream, cardamom and cloves. Bring to a boil over high heat, reduce heat to medium and boil gently, stirring often (at least every 5 minutes) and stirring in any skin that forms, until liquid is reduced to 3 cups (750 mL), about 80 to 100 minutes.

2 Place a sieve over a large measuring cup and strain. Discard solids. Return mixture to saucepan. Stir in sugar, almonds and pistachios; simmer over low heat, stirring, for 5 minutes. Remove from heat and set aside to cool.

3 Transfer mixture to a bowl. Place in freezer and chill, stirring a few times, until slushy, about 1¹/₂ to 2 hours. Whisk until smooth and thick. Spoon into molds, tapping them on work surface to remove any air pockets. Insert sticks and freeze until solid, at least 3 more hours.

Tip

I like to fortify the milk with a little 10% cream to boost the milk-fat content just a touch, to approximate rich natural milk.

VARIATION

SAFFRON AND PISTACHIO KULFI ICE POPS: Reduce cardamom to 6 pods. Omit almonds and increase pistachios to ¹/₃ cup (75 mL). In a small bowl, using the back of a spoon, coarsely grind a pinch of saffron threads with 1 tsp (5 mL) of the sugar. Stir into kulfi at the very end of cooking. While kulfi mixture is cooling, stir it 2 or 3 times.

Quick Nut Kulfi
Ice Pops

MAKES ABOUT 2$^1/_3$ CUPS (575 ML) ◆ 7 TO 9 ICE POPS

Not everyone has the time and patience to make kulfi at home in the traditional manner, but there are several good ways to approximate its rich reduced-milk flavor and texture. Canned evaporated milk and sweetened condensed milk come to the rescue for cooks with less time.

Fine-mesh sieve

1 can (12 oz/370 mL) evaporated milk

1 cup (250 mL) whole or 2% milk

$^1/_2$ cup (125 mL) half-and-half (10%) cream

8 cardamom pods, crushed

2 whole cloves

2 tbsp (30 mL) chopped blanched almonds

2 tbsp (30 mL) chopped natural pistachios (skins rubbed off) or blanched almonds

$^1/_3$ cup + 1 tbsp sweetened condensed milk

1 In a large, wide, heavy-bottomed saucepan, combine evaporated milk, whole milk, cream, cardamom and cloves. Bring to a boil over high heat, reduce heat to medium-high and boil, stirring every few minutes and stirring in any skin that forms, until mixture is reduced by about one-quarter, 10 to 15 minutes. (Lower heat a little if mixture threatens to overflow.)

2 Place a sieve over a large measuring cup and strain. Discard solids. Return mixture to saucepan. Stir in almonds and pistachios; simmer over low heat, stirring often, for 5 minutes. Stir in condensed milk. Remove from heat and set aside to cool.

3 Pour into molds and freeze until slushy, then insert sticks and freeze until solid, for at least 4 hours. If you are using an ice pop kit, follow the manufacturer's instructions.

Tip

When buying cardamom, look for fresh-looking green pods (they fade with time); white pods are bleached and should be avoided. (Black cardamom is from a different plant species and is not used in sweet dishes.) When using them whole or to extract the seeds, crack cardamom pods with the side of a chef's knife.

Masala Chai
Ice Pops

MAKES ABOUT 3 CUPS (750 ML) ◆ 9 TO 12 ICE POPS

Outside of India, when most of us say chai, we really mean masala chai, or spiced tea. But in India chai just means "tea." Perhaps not surprisingly, this spiced milk-and-water mixture is perfect for an ice pop.

Fine-mesh sieve

5 thin slices gingerroot

3 peppercorns

3 cardamom pods

2 whole cloves

$1^1/_2$ cups (375 mL) milk

$1^1/_2$ cups (375 mL) water

$1^1/_2$ tbsp (22 mL) loose strong Indian, Sri Lankan or Kenyan tea

$^1/_4$ cup (60 mL) sweetened condensed milk

1 In a dry skillet over medium-high heat, toast ginger, turning occasionally, until slightly dry and a bit browned on both sides, 2 to 3 minutes. Place in a mortar with peppercorns, cardamom and cloves and pound until spices are roughly crushed. (You can also do this on a cutting board, crushing each ingredient separately with the side of a knife.)

2 Transfer crushed spices to a saucepan and add milk and water. Bring to a boil. Reduce heat, add tea and simmer for 4 minutes. Remove from heat.

3 Place sieve over a large measuring cup and strain. Discard solids. Stir in condensed milk and set aside to cool.

4 Whisk mixture until frothy. Pour into molds and freeze until slushy, then insert sticks and freeze until solid, for at least 4 hours. If you are using an ice pop kit, follow the manufacturer's instructions.

Hong Kong–Style Milk Tea
Ice Pops

MAKES ABOUT 3¼ CUPS (800 ML) ◆ 9 TO 13 ICE POPS

Many people in Hong Kong start their days with a cup of "milk tea" — usually sweetened strong black tea made creamy with condensed and/or evaporated milk. Even on swelteringly hot summer days, scalding milk tea is served as a midday refreshment. Some of us might prefer it in the form of a refreshingly cool ice pop.

3 cups (750 mL) boiling water

3 tbsp (45 mL) loose Chinese black tea (see Tip, right)

¼ cup (60 mL) sweetened condensed milk

⅓ cup (75 mL) half-and-half (10%) cream

1 In a large teapot or heatproof measuring cup, pour water over tea; set aside to steep for 5 minutes. Strain into a large measuring cup. Stir in condensed milk and cream and set aside to cool.

2 Pour into molds and freeze until slushy, then insert sticks and freeze until solid, for at least 4 hours. If you are using an ice pop kit, follow the manufacturer's instructions.

Tips

Substitute 6 tea bags for the loose tea.

You can also make this ice pop with Indian tea, such as orange pekoe, Darjeeling, or use any of the classic British or Irish blends.

Vietnamese Coffee
Ice Pops

Filtered coffee is very popular in Vietnam. It is brewed using small metal filters over individual cups or glasses. For making iced coffee, the filter is placed directly over a tall, ice-filled glass holding a generous amount of sweetened condensed milk.

---

2 cups (500 mL) filter/drip-brewed strong Vietnamese coffee (see Tips, right)

¹/₂ cup (125 mL) sweetened condensed milk

¹/₄ cup (60 mL) heavy or whipping (35%) cream

1 In a large heatproof measuring cup, whisk together coffee, condensed milk and cream. Set aside to cool.

2 Pour into molds and freeze until slushy, then insert sticks and freeze until solid, for at least 4 hours. If you are using an ice pop kit, follow the manufacturer's instructions.

Tips

In Vietnam, coffee is made with a blend of dark-roasted Arabica beans, much like French coffee, and more than often flavored with chocolate or cocoa, but in the North American Vietnamese community, New Orleans–style dark roast blended with roasted chicory has become the coffee of choice.

You can find imported Vietnamese coffee and New Orleans chicory coffee at Asian supermarkets. New Orleans–style chicory coffee is also available at many American supermarkets. Both are available by mail order.

Masala Coffee
Ice Pops

MAKES ABOUT 3 CUPS (750 ML) ◆ 9 TO 12 ICE POPS

Masala coffee is spiced coffee brewed with lots of milk. It is very popular in southern India as well as Malaysia, where there is a significant southern Indian population. I'm not a big fan of flavored or spiced coffees and teas, but this preparation is truly delicious. It's a natural for ice pops because it's creamy, spicy and rich — a fantastic and unusual pick-me-up.

Large coffee press or fine-mesh sieve lined with double layer of cheesecloth

1 stick (about 2 inches/5 cm) cinnamon

5 cardamom pods, crushed

4 whole cloves

1/2 whole nutmeg, lightly crushed

1 tsp (5 mL) finely chopped gingerroot

1 1/2 cups (375 mL) water

1/4 cup (60 mL) freshly finely ground coffee

1 1/2 cups (375 mL) milk

3 tbsp (45 mL) sweetened condensed milk

1 In a saucepan, combine cinnamon, cardamom, cloves, nutmeg and ginger. Lightly toast over medium heat, stirring occasionally, until richly fragrant, about 2 minutes. Add water and coffee, increase heat and bring to a boil. Add milk; when mixture returns to a boil, remove from heat (otherwise it will bubble over). When contents have settled, return to heat and again bring to a boil. When mixture bubbles up, remove from heat.

2 Pour into coffee press or cover saucepan and set aside to steep for 5 minutes. Press down plunger of coffee press or strain mixture through prepared sieve placed over a large heatproof measuring cup. Discard solids. Stir in condensed milk and set aside to cool.

3 Whisk mixture until frothy. Pour into molds and freeze until slushy, then insert sticks and freeze until solid, for at least 4 hours. If you are using an ice pop kit, follow the manufacturer's instructions.

Tip

Use a medium-dark or dark-roast coffee, preferably ground just before brewing.

Mango Lassi
Ice Pops

MAKES ABOUT 3 CUPS (750 ML) ◆ 9 TO 12 ICE POPS

With just a few manipulations, mango lassi, the popular Indian mango and yogurt drink, transforms into wonderfully delicious and rich ice pops.

Fine-mesh sieve

Blender

$1/2$ cup (125 mL) milk

8 cardamom pods, crushed, or scant $1/2$ tsp (2 mL) ground cardamom

2 tbsp (30 mL) brown rice, agave or corn syrup or liquid honey

$12/3$ cups (400 mL) chopped ripe mango

$3/4$ cup (175 mL) plain yogurt (see Tip, right)

Pinch salt, optional

1 In a small saucepan, heat milk and cardamom just until boiling. Remove from heat, cover and set aside to steep for 5 minutes.

2 Place sieve over a bowl and strain milk, discarding solids. Stir in syrup. Set aside to cool.

3 In blender at medium-high speed, purée mango, yogurt, a scant pinch of salt (if using) and milk mixture.

4 Pour into molds and freeze until slushy, then insert sticks and freeze until solid, for at least 4 hours. If you are using an ice pop kit, follow the manufacturer's instructions.

Tip

Use at least 2% yogurt or yogurt with a higher fat content for this ice pop. Greek-style or drained (thickened) yogurt also produces a good result. Non-fat or 1% yogurt can be used but will produce an icy rather than creamy result.

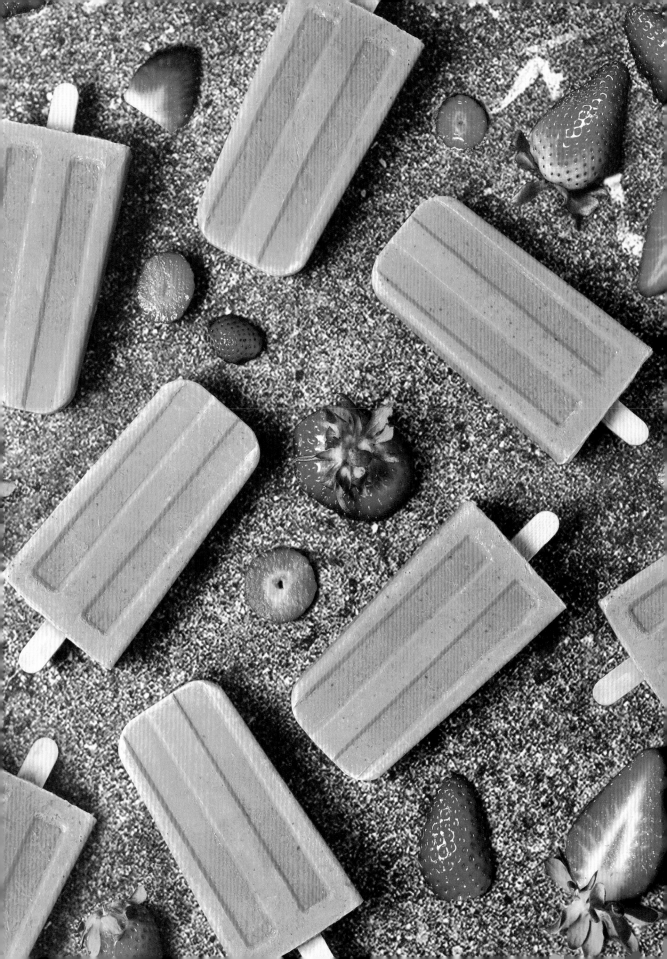

Strawberry Lassi
Ice Pops

MAKES ABOUT 2²/₃ CUPS (650 ML) ◆ 8 TO 10 ICE POPS

Honey and a touch of black pepper flavor these lassi-inspired ice pops.

Blender

2 cups (500 mL) halved hulled strawberries or frozen whole strawberries, thawed

1 cup (250 mL) plain yogurt (see Tips, right)

¹/₃ cup (75 mL) milk

¹/₄ cup (60 mL) liquid honey (see Tips, right)

Pinch freshly ground black pepper

1 In blender at medium speed, purée strawberries, yogurt, milk, honey and pepper.

2 Pour into molds and freeze until slushy, then insert sticks and freeze until solid, for at least 4 hours. If you are using an ice pop kit, follow the manufacturer's instructions.

Tips

It is preferable to use at least 2% yogurt or yogurt with a higher fat content for this ice pop. Greek-style or drained (thickened) yogurt also produces a good result. Non-fat or 1% yogurt can be used but will produce an icy rather than creamy result.

Use a light-flavored floral honey such as wildflower, orange blossom, acacia or clover.

Boozy

Negroni
Ice Pops

MAKES ABOUT 2 CUPS (500 ML) ◆ **6 TO 8 ICE POPS**

Like most cocktails, my favorite Italian aperitif, the classic Negroni, is too boozy
to freeze. Because it is usually garnished with an orange slice, I figured
we could incorporate all the flavors of the cocktail with its garnish,
in a sophisticated frozen orange "aperitif pop."

$1/4$ cup (60 mL) sugar

3 tbsp (45 mL) water

1 tsp (5 mL) finely grated orange zest

$1^3/_4$ cups (425 mL) orange juice
(see Tip, left)

1 tbsp (15 mL) gin

1 tbsp (15 mL) Campari

1 tbsp (15 mL) red vermouth

1 In a small saucepan, bring sugar, water and orange
zest to a boil, stirring until sugar is dissolved. Pour into
a measuring cup and set aside to cool. Stir in orange
juice, gin, Campari and vermouth.

2 Pour into molds and freeze until slushy, then insert
sticks and freeze until solid, for at least 4 hours or
preferably overnight. If you are using an ice pop kit,
follow the manufacturer's instructions.

Tip

Freshly squeezed orange juice is always best, but you
can also use juice from cartons or from concentrate.

Minty Campari Sunset
Ice Pops

MAKES ABOUT 2 CUPS (500 ML) ◆ **6 TO 8 ICE POPS**

As in Negroni Ice Pops, the bitter and sweet flavors of Campari pair nicely
with orange juice. Here I've added a cool accent of fresh mint.
For an English garden-party version, use the Pimm's.

$1/4$ cup (60 mL) fresh mint leaves

1 tbsp (15 mL) granulated sugar

$1^3/4$ cups (425 mL) orange juice

$1/3$ cup (75 mL) freshly squeezed lime juice

$1/2$ cup (125 mL) Campari or Pimm's No. 1 Cup

1 Chop or tear mint leaves into 3 or 4 pieces each, place in a measuring cup and sprinkle with sugar. With a muddler, pestle or the back of a wooden spoon, crush mint and sugar until leaves are well bruised and broken up. Stir in orange and lime juices.

2 Pour Campari evenly into each mold, using either six $1/3$-cup (75 mL) molds or eight $1/4$-cup (60 mL) molds. Pour juice mixture gently into molds. Freeze until slushy, then insert sticks and freeze until solid, for at least 4 hours or preferably overnight. If you are using an ice pop kit, follow the manufacturer's instructions.

Strawberry Daiquiri
Ice Pops

MAKES ABOUT 2 CUPS (500 ML) ◆ 6 TO 8 ICE POPS

Frozen daiquiris transform quite naturally into ice pops.

Blender

$1/_4$ cup (60 mL) water

$1/_4$ cup (60 mL) granulated sugar

$1/_4$ tsp (1 mL) finely grated lime zest

3 cups (750 mL) halved hulled fresh strawberries or whole frozen strawberries, thawed

3 tbsp (45 mL) white rum

3 tbsp (45 mL) freshly squeezed lime juice

1 In a small saucepan, bring water, sugar and lime zest to a boil, stirring until sugar is dissolved. Simmer for 1 minute, then set aside to cool.

2 In blender at medium speed, purée strawberries, rum, lime juice and reserved sugar syrup.

3 Pour into molds and freeze until slushy, then insert sticks and freeze until solid, for at least 4 hours or preferably overnight. If you are using an ice pop kit, follow the manufacturer's instructions.

Peach Daiquiri
Ice Pops

MAKES ABOUT 2 CUPS (500 ML) ◆ 6 TO 8 ICE POPS

The beautiful summer flavor of sweet ripe peaches, emphasized
with a splash of peach schnapps, makes a fine and unusual daiquiri ice pop.

Blender

3 tbsp (45 mL) water

3 tbsp (45 mL) granulated sugar

$1/4$ tsp (1 mL) finely grated lime zest

$2^1/_2$ cups (625 mL) chopped peeled ripe peaches (see Tips, right)

3 tbsp (45 mL) amber or white rum

$1/4$ cup (60 mL) freshly squeezed lime juice

2 tbsp (30 mL) peach schnapps

1 In a small saucepan, bring water, sugar and lime zest to a boil, stirring until sugar is dissolved. Simmer for 1 minute. Remove from heat and set aside to cool.

2 In blender at medium-high speed, purée peaches, rum, lime juice, schnapps and reserved sugar syrup.

3 Pour into molds and freeze until slushy, then insert sticks and freeze until solid, for at least 4 hours or preferably overnight. If you are using an ice pop kit, follow the manufacturer's instructions.

Tips

You can also use thawed frozen peaches or drained canned peaches for this recipe. If using canned peaches, replace the water and sugar with $1/_3$ cup (75 mL) syrup from the can.

Truly ripe peaches should be easy to peel with the side of a sharp knife blade. If, however, the skin is a bit tight, simply plunge the peaches in boiling water for about 10 seconds to loosen the skins.

Fruity Rum Punch
Ice Pops

MAKES ABOUT 2^1/$_2$ CUPS (625 ML) ◆ 7 TO 10 ICE POPS

Citrus, pineapple and strawberries make an unusual
but vibrant punch base for these ice pops.

Blender

^{1}/$_3$ cup (75 mL) water

3 tbsp (45 mL) granulated sugar

^{1}/$_2$ tsp (2 mL) finely grated
orange zest

^{1}/$_4$ tsp (1 mL) finely grated lime zest

1 cup (250 mL) orange juice

1 cup (250 mL) chopped pineapple

1 cup (250 mL) halved hulled fresh
strawberries or whole frozen
strawberries, thawed

3 tbsp (45 mL) freshly squeezed
lime juice

^{1}/$_4$ cup (60 mL) amber rum

2 tbsp (30 mL) grenadine syrup
(see Tips, left)

Dash angostura bitters (see Tips,
right)

1 In a small saucepan, combine water, sugar and
orange and lime zest. Bring to a boil, stirring until sugar
is dissolved. Reduce heat and simmer for 2 minutes.
Remove from heat and set aside to cool.

2 In blender, purée orange juice, pineapple, strawberries
and lime juice. Stir in rum, grenadine, cooled sugar
syrup and bitters.

3 Pour into molds and freeze until slushy, then insert
sticks and freeze until solid, for at least 4 hours or
preferably overnight. If you are using an ice pop kit,
follow the manufacturer's instructions.

Tips

Grenadine syrup is a clear red syrup originally made from
pomegranates (grenades in French) and now often from
a combination of red fruit flavorings. Look for it in
well-stocked supermarkets or liquor stores.

Angostura bitters are available at large grocery stores
as well as many liquor stores. It is a famous flavoring
produced in Trinidad. The original recipe, which
includes gentian and other herbs, was developed
in the Venezuelan town of Angostura.

Margarita
Ice Pops

MAKES ABOUT 2 1/4 CUPS (550 ML) ◆ **6 TO 9 ICE POPS**

This frozen Margarita is a true classic.

---

1 1/3 cups (325 mL) water

1/4 cup (60 mL) granulated sugar

2 strips (each 1/2 by 2 inches/1 by 5 cm) lime zest

Pinch salt

2/3 cup (150 mL) freshly squeezed lime juice

3 tbsp (45 mL) gold or white tequila

1 1/2 tbsp (22 mL) orange liqueur, such as Cointreau or Triple Sec

1 In a small saucepan, combine water, sugar, lime zest and salt. Bring to a boil, reduce heat and simmer for 2 minutes. Pour into a measuring cup and set aside to cool. Discard lime zest. Stir in lime juice, tequila and liqueur.

2 Pour into molds and freeze until slushy, then insert sticks and freeze until solid, for at least 4 hours or preferably overnight. If you are using an ice pop kit, follow the manufacturer's instructions.

Tip

Always use freshly squeezed lemon juice or lime juice in your ice pops; bottled just doesn't compare.

Tequila Sunrise
Ice Pops

MAKES ABOUT 2^1/$_4$ CUPS (550 ML) ◆ **6 TO 9 ICE POPS**

*Grenadine syrup mimics the red flash of emerging
sunlight in these delicious ice pops.*

---

^{1}/$_2$ tsp (2 mL) finely grated lime zest

3 tbsp (45 mL) granulated sugar

3 tbsp (45 mL) water

1^1/$_2$ cups (375 mL) orange juice

3 tbsp (45 mL) freshly squeezed
lime juice

3 tbsp (45 mL) gold or white tequila

2 tbsp (30 mL) grenadine syrup
(approx.)

1 In a small saucepan, bring lime zest, sugar and water to a boil. Reduce heat and simmer for 2 minutes. Pour into a large measuring cup and set aside to cool. Whisk in orange juice, lime juice and tequila.

2 Pour about 1 tsp (5 mL) grenadine into each ice pop mold. Very slowly and gently, pour orange mixture down the side into molds. Freeze until slushy, then insert sticks and freeze until solid, for at least 4 hours or preferably overnight. If you are using an ice pop kit, follow the manufacturer's instructions.

Tip
Grenadine syrup is a clear red syrup originally made from pomegranates (grenades in French) and now often from a combination of red fruit flavorings. Look for it in well-stocked supermarkets or liquor stores.

Whiskey Sweet-and-Sour
Ice Pops

MAKES ABOUT 2$\frac{1}{4}$ CUPS (550 ML) ◆ 6 TO 9 ICE POPS

Another classic American cocktail, the Whiskey Sour is a natural
base for an ice pop. It just needed to be sweetened up a bit.

Fine-mesh sieve

$\frac{1}{4}$ cup (60 mL) granulated sugar

1 tsp (5 mL) finely grated lemon zest

$\frac{1}{4}$ cup (60 mL) boiling water

1 cup (250 mL) orange juice
(see Tips, right)

$\frac{2}{3}$ cup (150 mL) freshly squeezed
lemon juice (see Tips, right)

$\frac{1}{4}$ cup (60 mL) Canadian or American
whiskey or bourbon

6 to 9 maraschino cherries, stems
removed

1 In a small bowl, mix together sugar and lemon zest,
rubbing together with the back of a spoon to muddle.
Add water, stirring until sugar is dissolved.

2 Place sieve over a large measuring cup and strain.
Stir in orange juice, lemon juice and whiskey of choice.

3 Drop one cherry into each ice pop mold. Pour whiskey
mixture into molds and freeze until slushy, then insert
sticks and freeze until solid, for at least 4 hours or
preferably overnight. If you are using an ice pop kit,
follow the manufacturer's instructions.

Tips

Freshly squeezed orange juice is always best, but you can
also use juice from cartons or from concentrate. In this
recipe, if you do not have enough after juicing the zested
orange, top off the quantity with prepared juice.

Always use freshly squeezed lemon juice or lime juice
in your ice pops; bottled just doesn't compare.

Red Greyhound
Ice Pops

MAKES ABOUT 2 CUPS (500 ML) ◆ **6 TO 8 ICE POPS**

Vodka and grapefruit juice make a classic Florida cocktail known
as the Greyhound. Here I've used gin instead of vodka and added
a blush of red with grenadine and sweet vermouth.

$1^3/_4$ cups (425 mL) red grapefruit juice

3 tbsp (45 mL) gin

2 tbsp (30 mL) red (sweet) vermouth

$1^1/_2$ tbsp (22 mL) grenadine syrup

1 In a measuring cup, stir together grapefruit juice, gin, vermouth and grenadine.

2 Pour into molds and freeze until slushy, then insert sticks and freeze until solid, for at least 4 hours or preferably overnight. If you are using an ice pop kit, follow the manufacturer's instructions.

Paloma
Ice Pops

MAKES ABOUT 2¹/₄ CUPS (550 ML) ◆ 6 TO 9 ICE POPS

Mexico's second-favorite tequila cocktail freezes with amazing success.

---

1 cup (250 mL) water

¹/₄ cup (60 mL) granulated sugar

2 strips (each ¹/₂ by 2 inches/1 by 5 cm) lime zest

Pinch salt

1 cup (250 mL) grapefruit juice

2 tbsp (30 mL) freshly squeezed lime juice

¹/₄ cup (60 mL) white or gold tequila

1 In a small saucepan, combine water, sugar, lime zest and salt. Bring to a boil, reduce heat and simmer for 2 minutes. Pour into a measuring cup and set aside to cool. Discard lime zest. Stir in grapefruit juice, lime juice and tequila.

2 Pour into molds and freeze until slushy, then insert sticks and freeze until solid, for at least 4 hours or preferably overnight. If you are using an ice pop kit, follow the manufacturer's instructions.

Mint Julep
Ice Pops

MAKES ABOUT 2$\frac{1}{4}$ CUPS (550 ML) ◆ 6 TO 9 ICE POPS

As a nod to tradition, you could replace the usual wooden sticks
with silver spoons for these sweet frozen versions of the classic
Kentucky cocktail, which is customarily served in a silver cup.

---

2 cups (500 mL) water

$\frac{3}{4}$ cup (175 mL) granulated sugar

1 cup (250 mL) lightly packed mint
leaves (preferably spearmint)

$\frac{1}{4}$ cup (60 mL) bourbon

2 tbsp (30 mL) freshly squeezed
lemon juice

1 In a saucepan, bring water and sugar to a boil, stirring
until sugar is dissolved. Add mint and remove from heat.
Cover and set aside to steep for 10 minutes.

2 Strain into a large measuring cup and set aside to cool.
Stir in bourbon and lemon juice.

3 Pour into molds and freeze until slushy, then insert
sticks and freeze until solid, for at least 4 hours or
preferably overnight. If you are using an ice pop kit,
follow the manufacturer's instructions.

White Russian
Ice Pops

MAKES ABOUT 2 CUPS (500 ML) ◆ **6 TO 8 ICE POPS**

The coffee in this ice pop is a wake-me-up, while the vodka
and brandy make a settle-me-down combination.

$1^1/_4$ cups (300 mL) milk

$^1/_3$ cup (75 mL) sweetened condensed milk

$^1/_3$ cup (75 mL) espresso or strong coffee

2 tbsp (30 mL) vodka

1 tbsp (15 mL) brandy or amber rum

$^1/_2$ tsp (2 mL) vanilla extract

1 In a large measuring cup, whisk together milk, condensed milk, espresso, vodka, brandy and vanilla.

2 Pour into molds and freeze until slushy, then insert sticks and freeze until solid, for at least 4 hours or preferably overnight. If you are using an ice pop kit, follow the manufacturer's instructions.

Sangria
Ice Pops

MAKES ABOUT 3 CUPS (750 ML) ◆ **9 TO 12 ICE POPS**

Sangria, with its abundant fruit flavors, makes a natural ice pop.

1/3 cup (75 mL) granulated sugar

1/3 cup (75 mL) unsweetened apple juice

3 strips (each 1/2 by 2 inches/1 by 5 cm) orange zest

2 strips (each 1/2 by 2 inches/1 by 5 cm) lemon zest

2 cups (500 mL) red wine (see Tip, right)

1/2 cup (125 mL) orange juice

3 tbsp (45 mL) freshly squeezed lemon juice

2 tbsp (30 mL) orange liqueur, such as Cointreau or Triple Sec

1 In a small saucepan, combine sugar, apple juice and orange and lemon zest. Bring to a boil, stirring until sugar is dissolved. Reduce heat and simmer for 3 minutes. Pour into a large measuring cup and set aside to cool.

2 Discard zest. Stir in wine, orange juice, lemon juice and liqueur.

3 Pour into molds and freeze until slushy, then insert sticks and freeze until solid, for at least 4 hours or preferably overnight. If you are using an ice pop kit, follow the manufacturer's instructions.

Tip

Use a red wine that is unoaked (not aged in wooden barrels) or, at the most, only lightly oak-aged. The tannins from oak would be too strong with all the other flavorings.

Mulled Apple Cider Punch
Ice Pops

MAKES ABOUT 3 CUPS (750 ML) ◆ 9 TO 12 ICE POPS

Another frozen version of a warm winter treat!

---

3 cups (750 mL) apple cider (non-alcoholic)

3 tbsp (45 mL) packed brown sugar

1 small orange, thinly sliced

1 small lemon, thinly sliced

8 whole cloves

4 cardamom pods, crushed

1 cinnamon stick, crushed

1/4 cup (60 mL) amber or dark rum

1 In a saucepan, combine cider, sugar, orange, lemon, cloves, cardamom and cinnamon. Bring just to a boil, stirring until sugar is dissolved. Reduce heat and simmer for 15 minutes. Remove from heat, cover and set aside to steep for 1 hour.

2 Uncover and set aside to cool completely. Strain, discarding solids. Stir in rum.

3 Pour into molds and freeze until slushy, then insert sticks and freeze until solid, for at least 4 hours or preferably overnight. If you are using an ice pop kit, follow the manufacturer's instructions.

Acknowledgments

Once again I must thank my culinary and life partner, Camilo Costales, for all his help. Without his tireless shopping and kitchen assistance and, most important, his tasting and sound (albeit somewhat annoying!) criticisms, I would be unable to produce a book with such a broad scope of good, sound recipes.

I also must give thanks for the generous support of my many neighbors and friends, kids and adults, who helped to ensure that hundreds and hundreds of ice pops were duly consumed and who offered their valuable tasting notes too.

I would like to particularly thank all the responsible fruit growers of the world for their fabulous and inspiring produce, without which well over half of this cookbook wouldn't exist. And finally, thanks to the inner child in all of us who still finds the idea of ice pops exciting and fun!

Enjoy making, serving and eating these ice pops.

Index

N

O

Library and Archives Canada Cataloguing in Publication
Title: Awesome ice pops / Andrew Chase.
Other titles: 200 best ice pop recipes
Names: Chase, Andrew (Author of Awesome ice pops), author.
Description: Previously published under title: 200 best ice pop recipes. | Includes index.
Identifiers: Canadiana 20230572499 | ISBN 9780778807193 (softcover)
Subjects: LCSH: Ice pops. | LCGFT: Cookbooks.
Classification: LCC TX796.I46 C43 2024 | DDC 641.86/3—dc23